PUEBLO AND MISSION

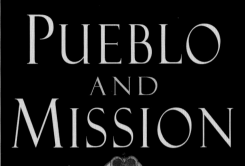

PUEBLO
AND
MISSION

CULTURAL ROOTS
OF THE SOUTHWEST

BY SUSAN LAMB

PHOTOGRAPHS BY CHUCK PLACE

NORTHLAND PUBLISHING

Para mi madrina, hermana Elizabeth Carey, IBVM, del condado West Meath, Irlanda, quien cruzó el océano para traernos amor.

— S.L.

These images are dedicated to my wife, Gerry, who allows me the freedom necessary to complete these long projects. I will always be grateful.

— C.P.

Text type set in Garamond
Display type set in Felix
Edited by Stephanie Bucholz and Jane Freeburg
Book design by Larry Lindahl Design
Production supervised by Lisa Brownfield
Manufactured in Hong Kong by Global Interprint

COVER, CLOCKWISE FROM UPPER LEFT:

Mission San Miguel, Socorro, New Mexico; restored kiva, Kuaua Ruins, Coronado State Monument, New Mexico; Hopi katsina dolls, Museum of Northern Arizona, Flagstaff, Arizona; Transept, Mission San Xavier del Bac, Tohono O'odham Nation near Tucson, Arizona

FRONTISPIECE / TITLE PAGE:
Ghost Ranch, Abiquiu, New Mexico

BACK COVER, CLOCKWISE FROM UPPER LEFT:
San Jose de Laguna Mission, Laguna Pueblo, New Mexico; San Carlos Apache Crown Dancers, Inter-Tribal Indian Ceremonial, Gallup, New Mexico; Great Kiva, Aztec Ruins National Monument, New Mexico; and bulto by santero Ernie Lujan, El Rancho de las Golondrinas, Santa Fe

Sources for all quotations and numbers for all artifacts in the collection of the Museum of Northern Arizona are listed in the Source Notes section, which constitutes an extension of this copyright page.

FIRST IMPRESSION
ISBN 0-87358-653-0

Library of Congress Catalog Card Number 96-39593
Cataloging-in-Publication Data

Lamb, Susan.
Pueblo and mission : cultural roots of the Southwest /
by SusanLamb ; photographs by Chuck Place.
p.   cm.
Includes bibliographical references and index.
ISBN 0-87358-652-2. — ISBN 0-87358-653-0 (pbk.)
1. Indians of North America—Southwest, New—History. 2. Indians of North America—Southwest, New—Social life and customs.
3. Indian calendar—Southwest, New. 4. Seasons—Southwest, New.
5. Southwest, New—Social life and customs. 6. n-ust. I. Title.
E78.S7L25 1997
979—dc21
                                                    96-39593

0581/7.5M/5-97

C O N T E N T S

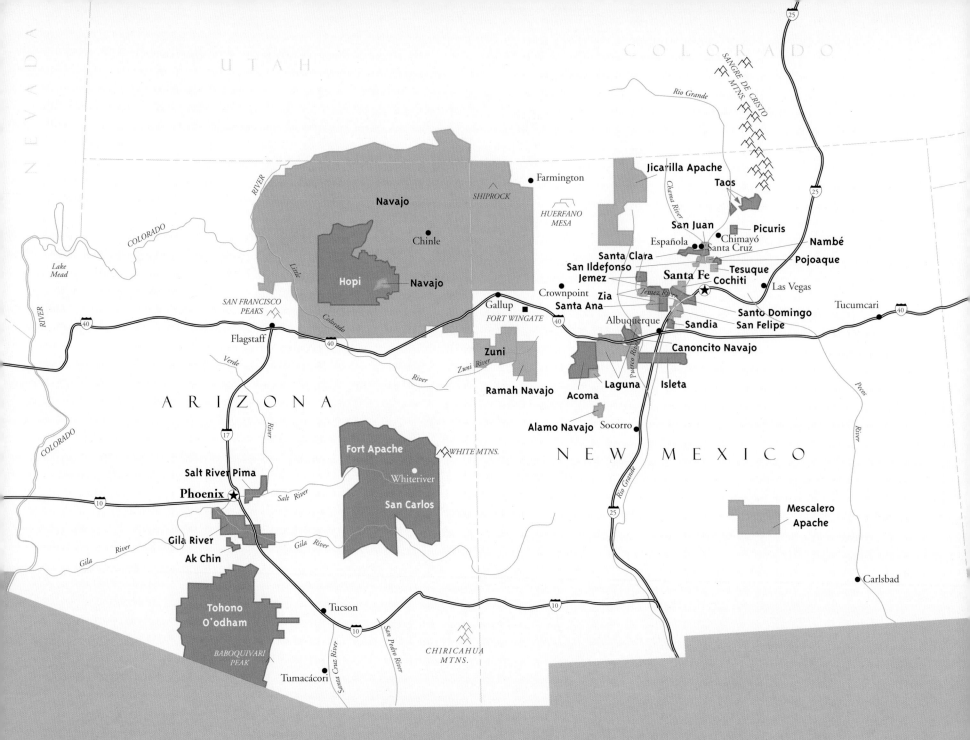

TRIBAL LANDS

of Pueblo and Mission

ACKNOWLEDGMENTS

"Everybody has their own point of view. Mine, of course, is mine."
— ERIC POLINGYOUMA, Hopi interpreter

CLUES TO UNDERSTANDING the Southwest are scattered everywhere here—in the landscape and the blossoming flowers, in the fierce storms of winter, and in the words of the people with whom we share it all. We each have our own view of this region that is colored by our own personalities, cultural backgrounds, and ideals.

I am grateful to all those who have been so generous, hospitable, and kind to me, a hopeful pilgrim. I would like to thank poet E. Almanza for our journeys together both actual and conversational, and Enrique Avendaño for his help with Spanish phrases. Michael Bird, Director of Preventive Health Programs for the Indian Health Service in Santa Fe, managed to be funny and disarming while explaining some sadly undeniable truths. Martha Blue willingly shared insights gained over a lifetime of working for justice for Native Americans. I am indebted to Geoff Bryce of the Taos Acequia Association for his synthesis of New Mexico water issues, to Father William Fitzgerald of Our Lady of Perpetual Help in Scottsdale, who introduced me to the concept of creation spirituality and whose joy in life is always contagious, and to Dr. Bernard Fontana of Tucson who was willing—as in several previous projects—to answer my naïve questions on short notice. Father Ed Fronske, OFM, of St. Francis Church in Whiteriver, taught me about learning from other spirits, whether they be two-legged or four-legged, finned or feathered. Jim Griffith of the Southwest Folklore Center gently batted around ideas with me from his highly original perspective. Doctor David Hurst of Denver helped me find my way through Jung, and Ann Kirkpatrick's sweet recollections of her childhood among the Apache introduced me to a thoughtful and gracious people. I also thank Danny Lopez of Sells, whose love of his culture and dedication to the future of young people are a model for us all. The Montoya family of Velarde showed me how it is possible to maintain faith and traditions while coping with the modern world. Tracy Murphy of the Museum of Northern Arizona helped with captions for the artifacts. Thanks to Leszek Pawlowicz of Flagstaff for sharing his knowledge of the stars and cyberspace, for finding such wonderfully obscure music, and for constructively challenging my assumptions.

I would also like to thank Charles Polzer, S.J., of the Arizona State Museum, who suggested that I look for connections between the agricultural cycle and the Catholic calendar. Thanks to the Polingyouma family of Kykotsmovi and Shungopavi, who over the years have taught me about Hopi ideals through their hospitality and humor. Ramon and Millie Riley of Whiteriver clarified several important points in regard to healing and about the beautiful Apache language. I am grateful to Alph Secakuku of Second Mesa, author of *Following the Sun and Moon: Hopi Kachina Tradition,* for his patient review of the manuscript and for his important comments. Thanks to Hazel and Robert Tohe, who looked over the manuscript with an eye to Navajo culture. I would also like to thank the good people of Our Lady of Guadalupe Parish in Flagstaff, who have always treated me as though I were their very own *hija.* I again enjoyed working with project director Janie Freeburg, a true Renaissance woman, and with Larry Lindahl and Kathleen Bryant who make everything they do a work of art. Stephanie Bucholz has been an unusually conscientious and considerate editor. As always, I am grateful to my husband, Tom Bean, for his understanding of the demands of fieldwork and deadlines and for his spirit of adventure, his open mind, and his ready wit.

Most of these people have full-time jobs, extended families, and considerable cultural responsibilities. Their willingness to introduce me to their world and to look over the manuscript was yet another example of how much they care about their own cultures and about humanity in general. Any errors of fact or interpretation remain, of course, my own.

— Susan Lamb

Images of artifacts, landscapes, architecture, and social dances were all used to illustrate the vast range of subjects covered in this book. Photography was inappropriate during certain ceremonies, however, due to their sacred nature.

As noted art historian Vincent Scully wrote in *Pueblo: Mountain, Village, Dance* (The University of Chicago Press) about restrictions on the photographing of Pueblo ceremonies:

> *I approve of the restrictions in any event. We can only be glad that the surviving Americans became so canny at last. Otherwise, one is soon doing it for the camera rather than for the god, and that is the end of it all.*

Our thanks must go to the Museum of Northern Arizona for allowing us access to their extensive collection of Native American artifacts and to El Rancho de las Golondrinas for making us welcome during their Living History Day. Many thanks also to Nathaniel Chee and the Mescalero Apache Nation for allowing us to photograph the dances held during their spring Mescal Roast. A number of individuals at parks, galleries, and trading posts were most generous with their time and information. Finally, special thanks are owed to Navajo weaver Sarah Natani for sharing both her art and her culture with us.

— Chuck Place

OLLA PODRIDA

"Man can be assimilated by a country. There is an *x* and
a *y* in the air and in the soil of a country, which slowly permeate
and assimilate him to the type of the aboriginal inhabitant."

— CARL GUSTAV JUNG, *Civilization in Transition*

EVER SINCE EUROPEANS ARRIVED in the Southwest, natives and newcomers have battled and blessed, ignored and influenced one another. Yet in contrast to the prevailing notion that native cultures have been utterly vanquished, the indigenous people of the region now encompassed by New Mexico and Arizona have not only maintained much of their own characters but have also strongly influenced the other cultures around them. Customs introduced by early colonists from Europe also endure, often alongside or blended with native ways of seeing and doing things. Today, the Southwestern way of life is a rich mix of traditions. Ages-old responses to land, community, and the cycle of seasons continue even in these modern times. From architecture to cuisine, agriculture to the arts, the persistence of these traditions is a testament to how appropriate they remain for life here.

When we encounter an expression of one of these cultures—a Hopi katsina doll or a Corn Dance at San Juan Pueblo, an exquisite O'odham basket or a humble adobe home—we understand intuitively that there is more to its appeal than the skill of the artist, performer, or builder. Just as we know that human beings are more than the sums of their cells and synapses, we feel that there is more to a Zia pot than molded clay, paint, and an oxidizing fire. We sense

Hano polychrome jar by
Fanny Nampeyo, Museum
of Northern Arizona

1

that despite the monumental, ongoing struggles between different ways of life in the Southwest, something extraordinary is alive here. Ask any member of a long-established Southwestern culture about this extraordinary "something," and they will tell you that it comes from paying close attention to matters of the spirit and living so intimately with the land that its seasons are felt in the heart.

THE PEOPLE

"Cultural diversity is an important world resource, as essential to the resilience of the human race in the long run as is biological diversity."

— DR. DAVID MAYBURY-LEWIS
anthropologist, Harvard University

Of the myriad cultures in New Mexico and Arizona that have persisted since the time of contact with Europeans, four groups are especially significant in the context of this book for their distinctive ways of life and their enduring influence. Today, they are most commonly referred to as the Pueblo, the O'odham, the Apache, and the Navajo. Within each of these broad groups, there are further differences that have grown out of smaller communities' specific environments and local histories. And of course each person in every community is an individual who expresses not only a tribal, but a personal identity.

For traditional cultures in general, though, family and community are paramount and individual freedom is never to be pursued at the expense of other people. Instead, a person's potential is fulfilled in terms of duty and respect for others and for creation. Through rich ceremonials, the native people of the Southwest both acknowledge and transcend the everyday realities of the world. Originally without a written language, they have always taught about life through song or the spoken word. Their land is known deeply, and every mountain, stream, and mesa bears a host of stories that have profound meaning and value for the cultures that tell them. Even those native people who live and work in cities—whether they are a high school teacher, a secretary, a lawyer, or a cook—often return to their villages at times of celebration or whenever their communities may need them.

THE PUEBLO PEOPLE

"This is a hard place to live—once in the sense of physical survival, now in the sense of spiritual survival. But it's a place that is supposed to challenge us, to separate the weak from the strong. It's made us who we are; it's made us tough. We're grateful for that."

— LANCE POLINGYOUMA
Hopi interpreter

Long ago when rainfall was apparently more dependable, Pueblo farming communities lay scattered across the Southwest. But during an extended drought at the end of the thirteenth century, many people abandoned their former villages. Hopi people settled around mesas in what is now northern Arizona, the Zuni along the Zuni River, and other

Pueblo cultures—their ceremonies, shared walls, and traditions—date back many centuries, yet have continually adapted and evolved. *Clockwise from left:* Acoma rainbow dancer and Zuni white buffalo dancers, Gallup Inter-Tribal Indian Ceremonial, Gallup, New Mexico; Zia *olla* (jar), Museum of Northern Arizona; Main plaza, Taos Pueblo, New Mexico

4

Hopi katsina dolls,
Museum of Northern
Arizona. Cow or *Wakas*
(from Spanish *vaca*)
katsinam joined
Hopi ceremonies after
Spanish settlers intro-
duced cattle. Wolf or
Kwewu (Hopi rendition of
a howl) katsinam repre-
sent creatures eliminated
from New Mexico and
Arizona by Europeans;
ironically, hundreds of
wolves still roam the
mountains of Spain.

Pueblo people along the Rio Grande and its tributaries that flow from the southern Rockies of New Mexico. Pueblo people believe that they were destined to migrate to various places in this way, learning valuable truths before settling in preordained homelands.

Pueblo is the Spanish word for "people" or "village," and is used as an umbrella term for the various members of this community-minded culture. Altogether, there are twenty Pueblo nations speaking dialects of six different languages from four separate linguistic families. Each pueblo has its own name for itself, although several are now generally known by the names of saints introduced by Spanish-speaking missionaries. Considering their individual histories, it is not surprising that there are many other differences between the pueblos. For example, property in the matrilineal western pueblos is held by women; in the eastern pueblos, descent is reckoned on the father's side and men own the property. Pueblos are organized by clans in the west, while Keresan pueblos are based on four ceremonial societies and still others are divided into two ceremonial *moieties,* or complementary halves. Yet in centuries of adapting to a daunting climate and landscape, the various Pueblos have also converged in many ways, epitomizing the Southwest as much as does a yucca plant or a juniper tree.

Living in stone or adobe villages at elevations of over a mile, where rain may not fall for months and it can freeze almost any night of the year, Pueblo farmers successfully coax corn of various colors, beans of different kinds, melons, and hard squashes from the land while endeavoring to maintain harmony with it and with one another.

One might imagine that such a difficult life would sap a culture's vitality, but just the opposite has been true. Every aspect of Pueblo life is full of purpose and carried out with minute attention to detail. There are songs, prayers, and blessings for every activity of the day and season of the year: for farming, hunting, and preparing food; for weaving, woodcarving, and potterymaking. Ancient, complex ceremonies mark the many passages of life from birth to death, including marriage and a series of initiations into different religious societies.

The Pueblo people are well known for their beautiful religious dances. These are intended to reciprocate for blessings, especially the rain and snow, and to express the human responsibility for maintaining balance and peace in the world. Whether a dancer or an observer, everyone present at a dance endeavors to be grateful, humble, and serene so that their good thoughts and kindly intentions will mingle into a powerful prayer for the welfare of all mankind.

Each pueblo has its own sacred rituals, meditations, and prayers. In western pueblos, at least half of the year is dedicated to *katsinam,* spirit intermediaries who were ritually invited to the pueblos after the great drought of the late thirteenth century. Aspects of the "old religion" that existed before the arrival of the katsinam complete the western ceremonial cycle. A few eastern pueblos do not include katsinam in their world view at all. Outsiders may be permitted to witness very old ceremonies in western pueblos but in the east, the most sacred old devotions are carried out in secret. Most pueblos—with the clear exception of Hopi—have blended practices of Roman Catholicism into their public celebrations. Pueblos on the eastern fringe also had considerable contact with tribal cultures of the Great Plains and adopted certain Plains traditions, especially in decoration and dancing.

THE O'ODHAM

"We don't say 'good morning.' Well, now there's a way to say it in O'odham, but we never used to say it. Everybody just knows it's a good morning. Things like that are understood."

— DANNY LOPEZ
Tohono O'odham educator

O'odham means "the people" in their Piman language. The soft-spoken O'odham live in the Sonoran Desert, a formidable environment indeed. While it may rain as much as fifteen inches per year in the eastern part of the Sonoran Desert, rainfall is just zero to five inches in its western reaches. With temperatures routinely exceeding a blinding one hundred degrees, it would be foolish to barge boisterously through the cactus and thorny mesquite of this desert in midday. Perhaps that is why O'odham people tend to be subtle and understated in both word and action.

The O'odham have always been masters of diversification, coping in different ways depending upon where they live. Before Europeans came, extended families of *Tohono* (Desert) O'odham—whom Spanish explorers dubbed *Papago,* from *bawi,* the O'odham word for tepary beans—

grew teparies, squash, and corn at the mouths of washes with the help of summer rains. They lived near mountain springs in winter. These O'odham knew their land well and could name around three hundred species of wild plants, forty of which were important food sources. They gathered mesquite beans, cactus fruit, roots, greens, and wild honey, and hunted rabbits, deer, and desert sheep.

Akimel (River) O'odham, or *Pima,* lived all year in thatch villages along permanent streams to the north, east, and south of their desert cousins. They farmed nineteen different domesticated plants including corn, tepary beans, cotton, squash, and chiles, and irrigated them by means of canals diverting water from streams. They hunted, netted fish from the rivers, and wove cotton cloth and baskets, which they traded for hides and salt. Spanish soldiers apparently called them *Pima* based on the O'odham term *pi ma:c,* meaning "I don't know," which may have been the answer to a question asked in Spanish—a language they didn't speak—perhaps: "What do you call yourselves?"

Like the Pueblo people, the O'odham have handed down ancient stories telling of a period of turmoil in their world that taught them great lessons about how to live together in the desert. Ethnologists find this refrain in cultural lore from all over the Southwest. Correlating the stories with archaeological evidence, many scholars see widespread upheavals in the region during the centuries preceding the even more cataclysmic arrival of Spanish soldiers. Possible causes include extended droughts, incursions of other people native to North America, and plagues carried to crowded villages along ancient trade routes. The ancestors of both the

6

Saguaro cactus grow about a foot every fifteen years and may live as long as two centuries. Their wreaths of waxy blossoms emerge in June, developing fruit by late July. Sonoran Desert people regard them as fellow humans rooted in place, their limbs upraised beseeching the sky for rain.

Pueblo and the O'odham shifted their settlements during these turbulent times, and adapted their religions to the changes in their circumstances.

Although in their difficult desert world they created less in the way of material culture than the Pueblo, the O'odham developed an elaborate non-material culture. Song is their great art form, "song-dreamers" their most admired members. An O'odham shaman is a genius of song, but not all song-dreamers are shamans or medicine men. Shamans once enhanced the power of the O'odham in battles, ensured good weather and successful hunts, and cured the sick. They have included both men and women in whose

dreams birds and other spirit guides explain how to control the great power that emanates from the earth. Although the O'odham integrated Catholicism into their lives and no longer look to shamans for most things, they still call for a shaman when they fall ill as a result of inappropriate behavior toward a powerful creature or place. There are also vestiges of ancient O'odham ceremonies based on the planting, growth, and harvest of corn.

The combined areas of the Tohono O'odham Nation make it the second-largest reservation in the country—about 2,700,000 acres—where about half of the almost seventeen thousand Tohono O'odham live today (the other half live mostly in cities such as Tucson and Phoenix). There are just over fifteen thousand Akimel O'odham. Much of O'odham culture is very fragile because it is not tangible or written down, but a few people still harvest cactus fruit, sing the old as well as new songs, and perform healing ceremonies. Today, dedicated teachers cultivate pride among O'odham youth in the traditions of their ancestors.

THE APACHE

"Good, like long life, it moves back and forth.
By means of White Water in a circle underneath,
 it is made.
By means of White Water spread on it, it is made.
By means of White Shell curved over it, it is made.
Lightning dances along it, they say."
— APACHE CRADLE CEREMONY SONG
transcribed by Chesley Goseyun Wilson

The more than fifty-three thousand Apaches of New Mexico and Arizona are mountain folk. It is not clear where the Spanish came up with the name Apache, but the people call themselves *Ndee* or "the people" in their own language, which is a form of Athabaskan linking them to native people in western Canada. Scholars disagree about when the Apaches arrived in the Southwest, but native musicologist Bryan Burton quotes a good Apache answer to this question: "We have been here since before the rocks grew hard."

Apaches were originally nomadic people. Upon marrying, men joined their wives to live in clusters of temporary brush homes called *wickiups* with other members of their new extended families. These matriarchal little communities foraged together from lowlands to mountains on a seasonal basis. For ceremonies or warfare, several families would band together and choose a nominal leader, whose authority lasted as long as he could persuade the others that his ideas were sound. Apaches were accomplished raiders who believed that anyone who had more than enough should share it or be willing and able to protect it.

The Apaches were not unified as one people; the survival of their families took precedence over every other consideration. Although there are large designations of Apaches today—the Jicarilla and Mescalero in New Mexico and the Western Apaches in Arizona—clan relationships are still the most important. This passionate attachment to family may be at the root of the Apache reputation for fierceness, as Apaches long sought violent revenge for any injury done a kinsman. During raids, Apaches concentrated on getting what they needed and avoided confrontations. Warfare was undertaken strictly for revenge. The object of war was to punish an enemy in the most devastating way imaginable. Battles were preceded and followed by fervent speeches and sensational dances acting out heroic deeds of vengeance.

Apaches also have the reputation of being able to make the most of whatever resources are at hand. All Apache groups adopted much from the bison-hunting cultures of the Great Plains. The Jicarilla, who settled in the cool, green mountains of northern New Mexico, also took on customs of their Pueblo neighbors there.

9

ANCIENT CALENDARS

"One must summer and winter with the
land and wait its occasions."
— MARY AUSTIN

IT IS OFTEN SAID that tribal people view time as
cyclical while European cultures view time as linear,
but this is not necessarily the
case. Any person who lives
close to the land is mindful
of the year's returning seasons,
and every culture tells stories
of its past.

Agricultural societies need
to know when to plant and
when to let their fields lie fal-
low. They need to keep track
of the seasons in order to honor
and propitiate the powers that
they believe determine the
success of their harvests. To do
so, they mark the movements
of the sun, which is so obviously the source of energy
that fosters growth. Farming
cultures (including those of
pre-literate Europe) have
usually taken note of the four
cross-quarter days—which fall
about mid-way between each solstice and equinox—
as key dates that represent each season's beginning.
The solstices and equinoxes are also important, for
they represent the heart of each season.

Southwestern farming cultures have long used
"calendar walls" to track these dates. The walls may
be part of a building as at Casa Grande, free-standing
as at Wupatki, or natural rock arrangements such as

Fajada Butte in Chaco Canyon or Hole-in-the-Rock
in Phoenix. Apertures in the walls frame various key
positions of the sun—such as sunrise on the morning
of the winter solstice—and are often linked to petroglyphs that symbolize their significance. In some
places, such as Hopi, villagers use topographical

Casa Rinconada, Chaco Culture National Historical Park, New Mexico

points on the horizon (depicted at right) or the position of sunbeams on the walls of their homes to keep
track of where the sun rises on certain days.

In addition to dates that are significant in
relation to the sun, native cultures mark time with
months of four weeks in accordance with the phases
of the moon (European farmers did the same long
ago). Because there are twelve and one-third of these

months in every lunar year, Pueblos add a thirteenth
month every three years in order to synchronize the
solar and lunar calendars.

Wandering societies need to know when to shift
to the high country for hunting and when to travel
down to forage in the deserts, as well as when it is
appropriate to perform cer-
tain ceremonies. The Apache
and Navajo year is divided
into two parts based on the
positions of constellations.
The six-month winter—
dominated by the sky—
begins in October, with the
appearance of the first of six
stars within a part of a constellation known as Thunder.
Each month, another star in
the constellation is visible.
The six months of summer,
assigned to the earth, begin
in April.

Stars are also used—
very precisely—as a watch
to mark the hours. A Hopi
priest may use the stars
wheeling in the sky outside
the kiva to orchestrate night-
time ceremonies. Apache *diyin* and Navajo *hataałii*,
both singers of sacred chants, observe the heavens
for signs and messages and can end ceremonies with
the appropriate song at sunrise because they know
the movements of the constellations so well. In
Canyon de Chelly, patterns of stars painted long ago
on nearly inaccessible rock overhangs express this
reverence for the night sky.

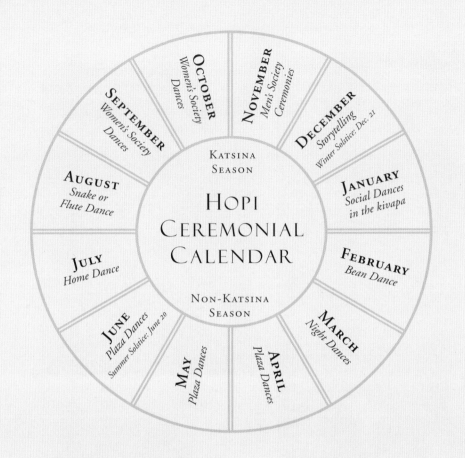

HOPI CEREMONIAL CALENDAR

Katsina Season

Non-Katsina Season

- **DECEMBER** — *Storytelling / Winter Solstice: Dec. 21*
- **JANUARY** — *Social Dances in the kivapa*
- **FEBRUARY** — *Bean Dance*
- **MARCH** — *Night Dances*
- **APRIL** — *Plaza Dances*
- **MAY** — *Plaza Dances*
- **JUNE** — *Plaza Dances / Summer Solstice: June 20*
- **JULY** — *Home Dance*
- **AUGUST** — *Snake or Flute Dance*
- **SEPTEMBER** — *Women's Society Dances*
- **OCTOBER** — *Women's Society Dances*
- **NOVEMBER** — *Men's Society Ceremonies*

KEY DATES ON EUROPEAN CALENDAR

These key events fall on or about the following dates:

NOVEMBER 2:
Cross-quarter day, beginning of winter.

DECEMBER 21:
Winter solstice, shortest day of the year.

FEBRUARY 2:
Cross-quarter day, beginning of spring.

MARCH 21:
Vernal equinox, day equals night.

MAY 1:
Cross-quarter day, beginning of summer.

JUNE 20:
Summer solstice, longest day of the year.

AUGUST 6:
Cross-quarter day, beginning of autumn.

SEPTEMBER 23:
Autumnal equinox, day equals night.

HOPI HORIZON CALENDAR

(FROM C. DARYLL FORDE, 1931)

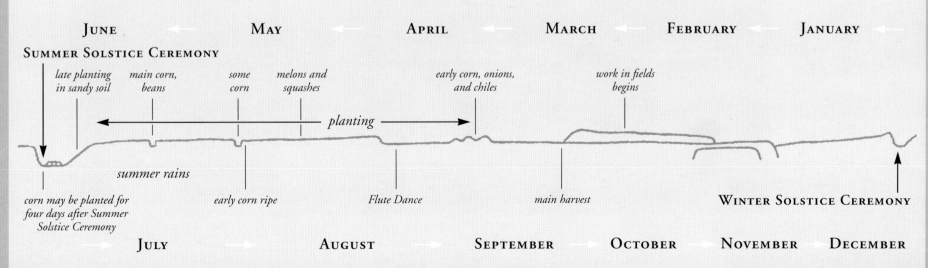

JUNE ← MAY ← APRIL ← MARCH ← FEBRUARY ← JANUARY

SUMMER SOLSTICE CEREMONY

late planting in sandy soil

main corn, beans

some corn

melons and squashes

early corn, onions, and chiles

work in fields begins

planting

summer rains

corn may be planted for four days after Summer Solstice Ceremony

early corn ripe

Flute Dance

main harvest

WINTER SOLSTICE CEREMONY

JULY → AUGUST → SEPTEMBER → OCTOBER → NOVEMBER → DECEMBER

12

Dancers at Apache Mescal
Roast, Living Desert Zoo
and Gardens, Carlsbad,
New Mexico. Apache
dance is lively and
individualistic and less
tightly choreographed
than that of other groups.
In what they wear, Apache
dancers often reflect
influences ranging from
the Plains tribes (feather
bustle) to the Spanish
colonists (cloth shirt).

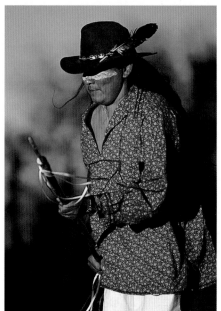

Traditionally, Apache children are trained to endure hunger, pain, and exhaustion. Custom allows both boys and girls great freedom but with many prohibitions that clarify respectful behavior in regard to power. In Apache belief, dreams and visions are vital in understanding one's place in the world and in leading a meaningful life. An Apache *diyi* (holy person) seeks to connect with forces innate in nature—animals and plants, lightning and mountains—to learn ceremonies needed to ensure the mental and physical well-being of the Ndee. Apache religion focuses on curing and preparation for warfare, and while the latter may seem irrelevant in these modern times, it is worth noting that the first American soldier killed in the Persian Gulf War was a young San Carlos Apache man.

THE NAVAJO

"The plants with colored blossoms are her dress.
It wears out. Yes, the earth's cover wears out.
The plants ripen and fade away in the fall.
Then in the spring when the rains come again,
Mother Earth once again puts on her finery."

— GEORGE BLUEEYES, hataalii
Between Sacred Mountains

"Navajo" is apparently from the Tewa Pueblo language and means "cultivated valley fields." Their own, Athabaskan name for themselves is *Dine'é*, "the people." Navajos may have arrived in the Southwest with the Apaches, but they separated at some point and the Navajo first settled on the

Detail, Navajo sand-painting, Broken Arrow Gallery, Taos, New Mexico. Traditional Navajo "sandpaintings" —actually images made of cornmeal, pollen, powdered flower petals, and charcoal as well as sand—are swept up after they have served to transfer the power of the Holy People to a person being cured in a ceremony.

13

Colorado Plateau in the northern reaches of New Mexico and southern Colorado. Their way of life was strongly influenced by Pueblo people, but certain of their nomadic Apachean habits—such as raiding—continued into the nineteenth century. Even though they have been established in the Southwest for four or five centuries, Navajos are still often described as "recently arrived" or "former nomads." Yet their world view is inextricably linked with the features of the landscape and, as a symbol of attachment to the land, a Navajo person's umbilical cord is buried at their place of birth.

Like their Apache cousins, the Navajo as a group have the reputation of being very adaptable to the circumstances in which they may find themselves. Anthropologists believe that they learned many strategies and customs from the Pueblos, such as how to farm corn and how to weave as well as aspects of ceremonialism, such as the carving of fetishes and sand painting. These practices, however, are ingrained in Navajo creation stories, which apparently predate their contact with Pueblo people. In any case, the Navajo are not village dwellers like the Pueblo, but live in homesteads of extended families—each with a matriarch at its heart—scattered across the landscape.

Navajo people consider the universe to be in perfect balance except when upset by human misbehavior. To cause injury or imbalance results in one's own illness or misfortune, and so Navajos endeavor to live in *hózhǫ́*, which loosely means a state of wholeness and harmony with all that is good and beautiful. Navajo ceremonies seek to restore this state of being, for to live without *hózhǫ́* causes mental and physical anguish. Based on tales of the supernatural *Diyin Dine'é*, or Holy People, most Navajo ceremonies take place as the need arises rather than on exact dates, though some are appropriate only in one season or the other.

The Navajo Nation has one of the fastest-growing populations in the country, almost a quarter of a million people with a median age of twenty-two. With over fourteen million acres, their combined reservation is the largest in the United States. The Navajo are great speechmakers and skillful politicians. (Since its inception in 1868, the reservation has been increased by the addition of about twenty large parcels surrounding the original block of land.) But like all people, the Navajo are individuals who may be more or less consistent with these generalities.

THE EUROPEANS

"Every white American who wants to know who he
is must make his peace with Europe."

— WALLACE STEGNER
Crossing to Safety

The Europeans who first ventured into the Southwest were by no means strictly Spanish. Historian Roger G. Kennedy points out that "from a military and administrative point of view, Arizona was a Basque province." Catalans, Italians, Portuguese, Greeks, Flemings, and Africans sailed to the Americas on Spanish ships as well. Later, Irish rebels against English authority, called "Wild Geese," joined Spanish military forces in the New World. Spain itself was composed

Spanish settlers brought writing and the wheel, adobe bricks and new crops, and metal for tools—but also for weapons. *Clockwise from top:* Nuestra Señora de Guadalupe de Halona Mission, Zuni, New Mexico; wheelwright shop and reenactment of loading a cannon, El Rancho de las Golondrinas, Santa Fe, New Mexico; 1850s-era family room, La Casa Córdoba, Tucson Museum of Art, Tucson, Arizona

of several kingdoms only recently unified under King Fernando of Aragon and Queen Isabella of Castile in 1479. It was a long-time "melting pot" of Celts, Romans, Visigoths, Vikings, and Moors. The Moors—a mix of Arabs and Berbers from North Africa—invaded Spain in 711 and ruled much of it until the Spanish toppled them in 1492. During those eight centuries, commoners as well as the Moorish and Spanish aristocracies intermarried with one another and with the families of Jewish court administrators. King Fernando himself was descended from all three groups.

We usually think only of soldiers and priests when we picture this incursion, but there were also servants, artisans, miners, farmers, clerks, and the adventurous younger sons of nobility. Many had traveled far in their lives, seen many kinds of people, and learned several languages. Their customs reflected diverse influences from North Africa, the Levant, and beyond, grafted onto regional European ways of life. Although their religious tradition stretched back thirty-five hundred years, it was in the process of being overwhelmed by scientific enquiry and leaps in engineering, mathematics, and astronomy. Metal, machines, and gunpowder gave many a new sense of power without a correspondingly updated moral imperative for restraint. Their sense of the world was powerfully shaken by events at home as well as experiences during their exploration of the "new world." Although both the Church and the Spanish crown considered native converts to be the equals of Europeans and theoretically eligible for the same rights and privileges, many soldiers and settlers saw no advantage in this view and ignored it.

The Catholic missionaries came from Italy, Switzerland, Germany, and other parts of Europe as well as from Spain. Dependent upon royal patronage, most were subject to the will of the Spanish monarchy. They varied in character, too—there were practical administrators, humanitarian friars, passionate intellectuals, and dreamy mystics in addition to the stereotypical Inquisitors. Some were progressives intrigued by the scientific advances emerging in Europe while others were appalled at the prospect of any change in the old ways of thinking. All were sent to teach of one God, whom they described as a god of love manifested throughout creation. They insisted upon the form of initiation known as baptism—and other sacraments such as marriage—as visible expressions of this faith. Like the complex ceremonies of the native people they encountered, their religious rites were steeped in tradition and symbolism and based upon the seasons of the year.

LA VENIDA (THE ARRIVAL)

> "And next morning I overtook four mounted
> Christians, who were thunderstruck to see me so
> strangely dressed and in the company of Indians.
> They went on staring at me for a long space of
> time, so astonished that they could neither speak
> to me nor manage to ask me anything."
> — ALVAR NÚÑEZ CABEZA DE VACA
> *Adventures in the Unknown Interior of America*

The people of New Mexico and Arizona knew a change was coming before they ever saw a conquistador, from stories circulated via their trading networks. Some Hopis say that the land told them, too, as strange plants migrated into their homelands ahead of the Spanish invaders who brought them to Mexico.

The first non-natives in what are now the southwestern United States were a Spanish soldier named Alvar Núñez Cabeza de Vaca and three companions who, shipwrecked on the eastern coast of Texas in 1528, were making their way to Mexico City on foot. It was a journey that would take them eight years. In the party was Estebanico, "a black Moor, a Native of Azamor," who had a gift for communicating in gestures with the native people. Around present-day El Paso, the men heard of prosperous farmers who lived to the north

along the upper Rio Grande. These must have been the Pueblo people, who no doubt soon heard of the scruffy strangers as well.

The four castaways continued west and south in the hope of reuniting with other Europeans. By the time they passed through O'odham country, they were escorted by dozens and often hundreds of native people, who apparently regarded them as shamans. But before they encountered Europeans on horseback, Nuñez and the others began to hear of Spanish depredations against the natives. The eagerly anticipated reunion deteriorated into a bitter disappointment. Núñez wrote:

> *And after this we had many and great altercations with the Christians, because they wanted to make slaves of the Indians we had brought; we were so angry. . . .*

A few years later, the Spanish viceroy of Mexico City sent Estebanico north with a small party, led by the Franciscan Fray Marcos de Niza, to investigate the people of the upper Rio Grande. Preceded by rumors of Spanish violence, Estebanico was killed when he reached the Zuni village of Hawikuh in 1539. His companions hid, but before fleeing back to Mexico they may have caught glimpses of the pueblo's walls shining like gold in the sun. Their report to the viceroy asserted that great riches were indeed to be found among the people to the north, and decried Estebanico's violent death.

So it was that Francisco Vásquez de Coronado entered New Mexico in 1540, at the head of an expedition of three hundred cavalry and foot soldiers supported by a thousand

native allies and bearers as well as several hundred pack animals laden with baggage and provisions. Three Spanish women went along, and six Franciscan friars accompanied the expedition in order that—as historian Marc Simmons notes from early documents—"The conquest might be Christian and apostolic and not a butchery." Whatever efforts the friars may have made were in vain, however. When the Zunis at Hawikuh resisted, Coronado and his soldiers crushed Hawikuh as well as pueblos near Bernalillo that refused to support the huge expedition all winter. Coronado made a futile search for gold, exploring as far as present-day Kansas and encountering Apaches living in wickiups on the *Llano Estacado*—the Staked Plains of eastern New Mexico and west Texas—before returning to Mexico.

The real and imagined wealth of the New World created many monsters among the conquistadors; missionaries and even other soldiers repeatedly protested their misdeeds. In 1573, King Felipe II of Spain promulgated ordinances that explicitly forbade the enslavement or abuse of native people and restricted Spanish settlement to "untilled" lands. But the conquistadors came from a blood-soaked period in European history and violent precedents were already thoroughly ingrained in the Americas. They continued to use incidents such as the killing of Estebanico to justify utterly subjugating the natives.

When an expedition under Juan de Oñate returned to colonize what is now New Mexico in 1598, King Felipe's ordinances made little difference to the Pueblos. Oñate established a headquarters at San Juan Pueblo and ordered raids on surrounding villages to support his colony. After

friars, colonists, and his own officers persistently objected to Oñate's methods, the viceroy replaced him with Pedro de Peralta. But the new governor not only continued Oñate's feudal *encomienda* system of exacting tribute from villages in exchange for "protection," he also conscripted Pueblos to build a capitol at Santa Fe.

Meanwhile, Franciscan friars established missions among the Pueblos and introduced European religion, music, agriculture, livestock, trades, literacy, and numbers. When Pueblo people resisted giving up their own religion, the friars imposed severe, medieval discipline on them. Spanish officers documented particularly harsh incidents in their ongoing battle with the Franciscans for control over the native people, who meanwhile were dying in heartbreaking numbers from introduced illnesses and demoralizing servitude.

REBELLION

"[Pueblos] mounted the first permanently successful American revolt on this continent, the only wholly efficacious Indian uprising. It is true that the booted men came back, but this time they came with considerable diplomacy, offering pardons, charters, and guarantees, most of which in this special instance have been more rather than less honored right up to now."
— VINCENT SCULLY
Pueblo: Mountain, Village, Dance
The University of Chicago Press

The lives of Pueblo people became intolerable. They labored for next to nothing under the encomienda system and there

19

were several drought-induced famines caused—the Pueblos believed—by the neglect of their ceremonies. In 1680, a San Juan man named Popé led a bloody revolt of all the Pueblos, including the Hopi people on their distant mesas. They drove out the Spanish soldiers and colonists—almost three thousand of them—and resumed their old ways. Their lives were already permanently altered, however, by new crops, livestock, and tools.

Spanish soldiers returned in 1692, but this time there were real changes in their policies and behavior. Although the Hopis again threw them out and some pueblos such as Jemez violently resisted them, their Reconquest was eventually achieved but on very different terms than before. For one thing, the Spanish authorities appointed a "Protector General" to look after the interests of the Pueblos. There were still incidents for which the clergy and military usually blamed each other, but the huge haciendas of the encomienda system were gone and in their place were smaller farms worked by individuals and their families. The colonists again depended heavily on the natives, but also reciprocated to some extent by coaching them in the care of cattle, sheep, fruit trees, and flowers new to the region, and in various trades. Recognizing the inherent contradictions and futility of their former approach, the Franciscans gentled their ways as well. Despite the bitter history of the seventeenth century, peaceful co-existence gradually evolved between the Pueblos and Spanish colonists. These bonds grew stronger as Apache and Navajo raiding increased and Comanche and Ute marauders—displaced by pressures elsewhere—swept in from the grasslands.

ARIZONA—THE NORTHERN EDGE OF SONORA

"I tried to reason with the lieutenant and advised him to go gently with the new people, but he defied me. We had several quarrels on the subject. Imbued with the spirit of military wantonness and aided by the soldiers, he paid no attention to my protests but meted out punishments right and left."

— JUAN MATEO MANJE
captain, *Compañia Volante*

Alliance against raids was also the glue that held the O'odham and the Spanish forces together in the southern part of what is now Arizona. In the late 1600s, Jesuit missionaries led by Father Eusebio Francisco Kino entered the area with a deliberately different approach and on a much smaller scale than the Franciscans in New Mexico almost a century earlier. A handful of Jesuit priests, usually escorted by a few soldiers and natives but sometimes alone, rode all over the Sonoran Desert preaching and baptizing, often giving away cattle, sheep, and pack horses laden with supplies. They learned the native languages and ate the native food. Over time, they founded missions along the Santa Cruz River where O'odham people began to concentrate, seeking food, shelter, and protection from Apache raiders.

Although there are large cities in the Sonoran Desert today, the isolation of this region at the beginning of the eighteenth century was profound. The Jesuits built churches in a few promising spots but were only able to visit them once or twice a year. Little by little, however, European

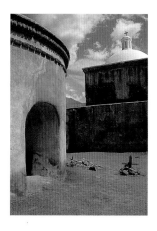
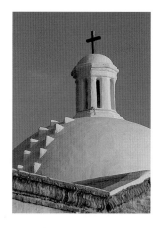

Tumacácori National Historical Park, Arizona. Established by Father Kino in 1691, Tumacácori is the oldest mission in Arizona. After the Pima Rebellion of 1751, the original church of San Cayetano was moved and renamed San José; the present church was begun about 1799. *Top, from left:* Mortuary chapel and cemetery; sanctuary dome; interior of sanctuary; bell tower

A rich mix of introduced
and indigenous elements
adds color and texture to
every facet of South-
western life. *Clockwise
from top left:* Indian
corn, El Rancho de las
Golondrinas; Zuni olla with
concave base for balanc-
ing on the head, Museum
of Northern Arizona;
snake-shaped door handle,
Mission San Xavier del Bac,
Arizona; detail of "Ganado
Red" Navajo rug, Museum
of Northern Arizona.

settlers and miners moved up along the rivers from the south, sometimes enslaving the natives to work in mines. Soldiers sent to keep the peace tended to favor the Europeans and life deteriorated for the O'odham as it had for the Pueblos. Again some missionaries and some soldiers objected, but again it took an uprising—this one led by Pima Luis Oacpicagigua in 1751—to get the attention of the authorities. The Spanish reconquest was milder this time, but the O'odham were not entirely pacified. As the Apaches stepped up their raids, the Spanish authorities established a garrison at Tubac in an unsuccessful effort to strengthen their control of the area.

Politics in Europe led to the expulsion of the Jesuits from all of the Americas in 1767–68. They had always maintained that they owed their first allegiance to their faith rather than to the crown, and had alienated colonial administrators, military officers, and colonists alike by defending the rights of native people. Father Kino, for example, enforced a *cédula* (document) protecting Indian converts from being enslaved, a real cause of resentment among the colonists. The Jesuits were replaced by Franciscan friars.

The Spanish Empire began to disintegrate in the late 1700s, leading to further isolation of its frontier communities. As their support from the crown withered away, fewer priests came to the Southwest and yet Hispanic, Pueblo, and O'odham villagers continued devotions that evolved over time into unique expressions of the Catholic faith. Hispanic colonists learned to make everything for themselves, including tools, rugs of wool dyed with local plants, and carvings for their churches. Natives, in turn,

became proficient at new skills from the tending of orchards and livestock to European trades, art, and music. Introduced customs—some held over from the medieval era, some a reflection of the emerging Renaissance—mixed with those of indigenous people.

Aftermath

"This synthesizing continues today, in contemporary efforts to combine the eternal verities of native life with the benefits and unavoidable impositions of the encompassing American and Hispanic societies."

— Alfonso Ortiz
anthropologist, San Juan Pueblo

Today, the pockets of traditional lifeways in Arizona and New Mexico are among the poorest places in the nation in terms of material well-being. The overall standard of living in New Mexico rivals that of Mississippi as the poorest in the country; about half of Navajo and O'odham people and a third of Pueblo and Apache people live below the federal poverty level. Yet in terms of landscape and culture, the rural Southwest is considered one of the richest parts of the United States. Visitors come from all over the world to savor the scenery and way of life here.

Although some indigenous traditions have teetered on the edge of extinction ever since the arrival of Europeans, most native people take a serious interest in the old, old ways. Whether they live on reservations or in towns, around three-fourths of Pueblo and Navajo people and about half of Apache and O'odham people continue to speak their own

23

languages, according to the U.S. Census. Most continue to observe their own religions as well. Some celebrate both native and introduced Catholic ceremonies, considering them "all ways of praying for a good life," or have simply added Christ to their own pantheon as one of many benevolent powers engaged in an ongoing struggle between good and evil. Over time, Hispanic Southwesterners have been influenced by the indigenous view of life as well, especially in their reverence for the land.

OLLA PODRIDA

"The Age of Exploration! In our school days, we were
told it was a time of heroes, and of high adventure.
Later, we came to understand what terrible suffering
and injustice the Spaniards had wrought in their
drive for fame, glory, and riches. . . . This recording,
nonetheless, has a different case to make: it pleads for
attention to the meeting places of light and beauty
that did indeed exist in those terrible, hard centuries."
— JOEL COHEN, conductor

In Spanish cuisine, there is a marvelous stew that is much greater than the sum of its parts. Redolent of elements one can't quite name, it can be a transcendent experience when the right seasonings are used, not the least of which is the time its mysterious contents spend simmering together. But if we could only see the cook holding her nose as she adds certain ingredients, we would fully appreciate the stew's name of "olla podrida," which literally means "putrid pot" in English. In much the same way, although many aspects of the European arrival appall us, the commingling of native and introduced cultures—in combination with the four and a half centuries they have spent together—has made the Southwest one of the most intriguing regions in the country. The old ways endure—generation to generation, season by season—reminding us all to be aware of the land and of each other.

Aspen trees and snow,
San Francisco Peaks,
Coconino National
Forest, Arizona, and
San Juan deer dance,
Gallup Inter-Tribal
Indian Ceremonial

24

WINTER

IN THE SOUTHWEST, THE LANDSCAPE SURMOUNTS ALL
CULTURAL DIFFERENCES. PERHAPS ELSEWHERE PEOPLE CAN
IGNORE WHERE THEY ARE, BUT NOT HERE. EVERYWHERE IN
ARIZONA AND NEW MEXICO, TRADITIONAL PEOPLE WATCH THE LIVING BODY
OF THE EARTH AND THE SEASONS AS THEY ADVANCE, ONE AFTER THE OTHER,

to claim it. Signs of winter—short days and frosty nights, withered plants, leafless trees, migrating game and birds— appear around the beginning of November. The sun's path is short and so low on the southern horizon that days are not long enough to sustain the growth of plants. Roots and seeds are dormant; the resting land lies bare and revealed.

As long as the weather permits, the onset of winter means drying and storing vegetables and seeds, culling herds, hunting, and preserving meat. The fairest days are sunny and calm, allowing time to replenish firewood and dry laundry before swirls of glittering snow sweep everyone indoors. Winter then becomes a time to distill the experiences

and observations of the past year: the lessons learned, the blessings bestowed. It is a time of reverence, thanks, and pledges to unseen powers, when people inwardly prepare for the year to come by renewing their bonds with the earth and with their communities through reflection and ritual.

Winter brings a watery blue tint to the diminishing hours of sunshine that divide long, cold nights. The day's heat dissipates quickly in the dry air after dark; temperatures plunge at sunset. Winter's dark nights offer brilliant views of the stars. Both Apaches and Navajos regard the constellations as models of harmonious behavior, and use them to mark the passage of the seasons. For example, the early evening position of the Pleiades star cluster at the beginning of November signals the imminent danger of frost. Winter is the proper season for the *Night Chant,* in which a Navajo *hataałii* (singer) leads his patient on a nine-night spiritual journey to overcome an injury, physical or otherwise. Such winter ceremonials embrace the dark and chill of the season, using both to explore and strengthen the human spirit.

Many O'odham families spend November 2 cleaning and decorating the graves of their forebears, chatting and sharing food with one another and with their departed relatives as their children run and play in the cemetery. Later that evening, guided by candles flickering in cups of colored glass, they make their way to feast with and honor their ancestors, lingering to reminisce, pray, and make peace with the year that is drawing to a close. In this way, O'odham and many Hispanic Southwesterners observe All Soul's Day.

This Day of the Dead—*El Día de los Muertos*—is a blend of ancient native traditions and Catholicism. Before the arrival of Europeans, various Mesoamerican people celebrated death as the soul's entry into another, more desirable realm beyond the trials of earthly existence. They held ceremonies in memory of the departed and took food and drink to their tombs. Apparently, missionaries standardized this practice by connecting it with the feasts of All Saints and All Souls. All Saints (November 1) is an occasion to honor all holy men and women whether or not their names have been formally recognized by the church, while All Souls (November 2) is a day to pray for departed relatives and friends. In turn, these feasts are based on old European customs prompted by the coming of winter. As the harvest ended and life became dormant, Celtic people believed there was an opening into the realm of the dead, who could visit and counsel the living on November 2, a cross-quarter day celebrated as Samhain, the Celtic new year. In other parts of Europe, the dead might bring gifts. In any case, indigenous and European feasts in honor of the dead combined into Día de los Muertos as it is celebrated today, which many consider the most important religious holiday in Mexico and those parts of the Southwest that have a strong Mexican or Mesoamerican influence.

Stringing chiles at El Rancho de las Golondrinas. Chiles strung in ristras to dry have become a symbol of New Mexico, which produces over 120,000 tons of chiles a year. More than a seasoning, chiles are rich in fiber and protein as well as vitamins. Eating chiles relieves congestion, while chile poultices ease arthritis and muscle pain.

Early November is also an important time throughout the Pueblos. In many places, fires are lit to symbolize hope for the renewal of life itself. Priests set the dates of ceremonial events for the coming year and pray for the regermination of all life: plant, animal, and human. Members of Hopi religious societies fast and purify themselves, and teach initiates their spiritual and social responsibilities. *Shalako*—giant couriers of the rainmakers—arrive at Zuni, pledging seeds and rain. Their visit is an occasion for feasting and dancing, one of just two times during the year when corn is ground between stones in the laborious old way.

BETWEEN EARTH AND SKY: LANDFORMS

"The enduring drama of the West is still a drama of sky and land. Thousands of pioneers recorded their sense of insignificance in relation to it, and many historians have observed that the pioneers were right: they *were* insignificant in relation to it."

— LARRY McMURTRY

Across northern New Mexico and Arizona, there is great variation in natural habitats. There are flat, grassy eastern prairies where once both Pueblos and Apaches hunted enormous herds of bison, and the forested southern Rockies of the Tiwa Pueblos and Jicarilla Apaches. The Rio Grande and its tributaries water lovely valleys—the realm of Tewa, Towa, and Keresan Pueblos—while snowmelt brings flowers to the massive, pine-clad mountains of eastern Arizona

where the Western Apaches now live. Dramatic red mesas and volcanic features punctuate the high plateau country of the Hopi and Navajo; ancient Pueblo ruins and shrines dot the upwarped region around the Grand Canyon. Below seven thousand feet, only sparse shrubs and grasses or scrubby piñon and juniper trees tint these landscapes green, though lines of cottonwoods and willows trace the courses of streams. The southern reaches of both states are varied, too: Cool mountains rearing up from the hot Chihuahuan desert of sagebrush, yucca, and agave are home to Mescalero and Chiricahua Apaches now; the O'odham live below the jagged fault-block ranges of Arizona's Sonoran Desert. Living in a land of such grandeur and hardship is humbling; surviving in such a difficult place cultivates an observant mind and a grateful heart.

On crisp winter mornings, landforms on the horizon loom dark and sharp even though spicy juniper smoke smudges the air like incense. Mountains and mesas make their presence felt every dawn. Everyone knows that clouds collect over such high places, and in winter drop snows that feed the streams of spring. As the snows fall, deer, elk, and other game animals emerge. Such uplands are deeply familiar to indigenous people and yet regarded as sacred. Certain mountains are especially revered by those who dwell in their shadows.

Mountain symbolism crops up everywhere in the Pueblo world—in architecture, on pottery, and in the spruce boughs worn by ceremonial dancers. Architectural historian Vincent Scully reminds us that Pueblo villages are a continuation of landscape forms and can "hardly be understood or sympathetically appreciated otherwise." Each pueblo especially

Clockwise from top left:

West Mitten Butte,

Monument Valley Tribal

Park, Navajo Nation,

Arizona; Baboquivari

Peak, Tohono O'odham

Nation, Arizona;

Sunset Crater National

Monument, Arizona;

Canyon de Chelly National

Monument, Navajo

Nation, Arizona;

Hesperus Peak, La Plata

Mountains, Colorado

30

reveres four of the mountains that surround it; these sacred peaks are amplified and included in pueblos by the shape and arrangement of buildings and open space. Simply standing in the abandoned plaza of Puyé, for instance— with its mountain looming up on one side and bluffs dropping away to immense vistas all around—one feels held aloft by the land. Truchas, Sandia, Taylor, Lake Peak, Taos:

Each of these mountains is a powerful, yet not oppressive presence in its pueblo. Hopi villages look to the distant San Francisco Peaks, capped with snow or wreathed in clouds much of the year, as the spiritual home of the katsinam, benevolent spirit beings.

Don Usner, whose ancestors go back three centuries in the Chimayó area, writes, "Walking in these hills, I've come to appreciate the Tewa notion that the hilltops are powerful intermediaries between the world of people and the world of the mountain spirits." Descendants of pre-Enlightenment Europeans who still believed the natural world to be suffused with the divine, Hispanic people in many little Southwestern towns consider surrounding hills and mountains to be sacred. White-painted wooden crosses top *cerros,* or hills, near northern New Mexico villages, drawing prayerful processions on holy days.

Ethnologist Ruth Underhill wrote of the Tohono O'odham: "As they climb into the hills, they do not speak, for noise always seems, to the Papago, to be disrespectful to the supernatural powers." The desert floor can be formidably hot, but the steep mountains are a cooler realm, often home to streams and trees, certain birds, and other creatures seldom seen in the desert. O'odham hunters still seek deer in the mountains after the corn has been harvested below. Baboquivari Peak is sacred to Tohono O'odham, for it is the dwelling place of *I'itoi,* Creator and Elder Brother.

Apaches hold that long ago, Yusin, the Creator, sent *Ga an,* spirits from the mountains, to bestow healing and blessing ceremonies on the Ndee. The *Ga an* set an example, teaching people how to live a Lifeway that is sacred. They taught them to listen to the trees and to feel the life beating within the rocks, never to put themselves above one another, take sole ownership of anything, or be so arrogant as to leave footprints on the ground. They taught them to dance, and Apaches still assume the identity of mountain spirits on certain occasions. *Ga an* dances are held to celebrate, to cure sickness, to ward off evil, or when there is a special need in

the community. The presence of the *Ga an* is a serious event, not an occasion for hilarity; as a show of respect an Apache never laughs in their presence. As the home of the *Ga an* and the source of powers both metaphysical and practical—such as healing herbs—mountains are an integral part of Apache spiritual geography.

It seems that every feature of the landscape where Navajo and Apache people live is enshrined in their creation story, in which a being named Changing Woman (White Painted Woman among the Apaches) gave birth to sons fathered by the sun. Called Monster Slayer and Born for Water, the twins traveled across the land, battling alien gods and demons who were making the earth unsafe. These Warrior Twins left pieces of monster strewn about as rocks and mesas, and pools of monster blood as hardened lava flows. Old stories relate an event for every setting: the walls of Narbona Pass crushed people passing through until the Twins propped them open; Monster Birds perched on Shiprock when not swooping off with humans to feed to their nestlings. Gobernador Knob is considered holy because it is where Changing Woman's parents found her after they emerged into this world from several previous ones. She and her sons were raised on revered Huerfano Mesa. Apaches and Navajos consider the mountains themselves—like other natural phenomena—to be not only sacred, but alive. Certain streams represent the veins of the *Diyin Dine'é,* or Holy People, who created this world and give it life, and who travel on rainbows and sunbeams. The Navajo world is bounded by four primary sacred mountains: Blanca Peak, Mount Taylor, the San Francisco

Peaks, and Hesperus Peak. Hataalii carry a little dirt from these mountains in prayer bundles, for they are their source of spiritual strength. The long winter Mountain Chant endeavors to clear away problems caused by disrespectful behavior towards mountains and mountain creatures.

AWAITING THE SOLSTICE

"Because the seasons really do require a sensible response from us, the pattern they impose means more than just a change in the weather. It means that some behavior is condoned, that other behavior is proscribed, and that an authority higher than ourselves—here symbolized by the natural order of the year—establishes what is right and what is wrong. Failure to act in congruence with the moral order is like a greedy search for apples in a blizzard. It threatens survival."

— E.C. KRUPP, astronomer
Beyond the Blue Horizon

The winter solstice is the moment when the sun reverses its retreat toward the southern horizon and begins its return to a welcoming people. Although the sun can seem a fierce adversary for much of the year, people who live on the land know that it is the source of light and warmth essential to the life of plants, animals, and humankind.

Pueblo people in particular prepare very seriously for this important day. The Hopi consider the month in which the solstice occurs to be the Dangerous Moon, because it is

when the sun will decide whether or not to come back again. Hopis fast and pray—not just for themselves but for all people—and recount ancient morality tales for adults as well as children. *Soyalkatsinam* visit villages to bless them with fertility and to observe what they need, which other katsinas will bring after the solstice itself. At Zuni, the initial coming of the Shalako is followed by fasting and prayer, and families make little clay effigies representing the good things they hope to receive in the coming year.

Winter celebrations and ceremonies also take place at other pueblos, many of them in private. Among the better-known public dances are those portraying game animals, which acknowledge and reciprocate for the gift of sustenance by deer, pronghorn, and bison. Dancers subtly imitate certain traits of the animals—such as the high foreheads of pronghorns or the synchronized movements of herds of deer—revealing an intimacy born of a respectful relationship maintained over centuries. It is also clear from these dances that Pueblo people mingled with the people of the Plains when they hunted there, for there is a Plains style to their movements and costumes. Although animal dances were once held only during the winter season, they may take place at any time of year now, often mixed with Catholic holidays such as the feast days of saints. At dawn on the winter feast of San Ildefonso in 1945:

As the song reached its climax, a long, grey plumed
serpent of smoke rose from the hilltop and spread over
the pueblo. From between the hills came the leader,
the hunters, the Buffalo lady and men. From over the

Mission San Xavier del Bac. In 1692, the Jesuit Father Kino founded his most northern missionary outpost at the O'odham village of Wa:k. Franciscans began construction of the lovely church of San Xavier, known as the "white dove of the desert," around 1776. While Spanish architects and artisans designed and ornamented the church, the O'odham built the structure itself.

Nacimiento by Maria Luisa Tena, La Casa Córdoba, Tucson. Following a custom begun by Saint Francis in 1223, many Hispanic households create a *nacimiento,* or nativity scene, for Christmas. These often depict not only the infant Jesus in the manger but also other Biblical scenes and scenes from daily life.

hills came Deer and Antelope and Mountain Sheep.
All came to the foot of the hill where the women
waited to touch them, where the chorus waited to
accompany them to the plaza with an exultant song.

December means the season of Advent to Catholics, who pray for peace in the world, give alms, and in other ways emphasize serving the poor for the four weeks leading up to December 25, when they will celebrate the birth of Christ. Endeavoring to keep a watchful and welcoming heart, Catholics believe that Christ may be found in small occurrences and in the least expected places. Advent, a season of hope, begins with Mass on the Sunday one lunar month before Christmas. This is the Catholic new year: the first day of the liturgical, or ritual cycle of the Church.

December 3 is the feast of Saint Francis Xavier, close friend of Ignatius Loyola, founder of the Jesuits. Xavier served as a missionary to the Far East in the 1540s, traveling thousands of miles under harrowing conditions to remote places. A figure of major importance to Jesuits, his feast day is joyfully celebrated at San Xavier del Bac and Tumacácori, which were both founded by this order of priests. An elaborate multi-cultural fiesta around the old ruined church of Tumacácori features the music, dancing, and food of O'odham, Apache, Yaqui (a people also native to the Sonoran Desert), Hispanic, and Anglo people.

December 12 is a day of special significance for Hispanic Catholics. It is the feast of Our Lady of Guadalupe, patroness of Mexico and the Americas and of towns from Phoenix to Tortuga to Pojoaque. It commemorates the vision of a Mexican native named Juan Diego, who in 1531 saw the Virgin Mary as a pregnant Aztec maiden with dark hair and skin and the moon at her feet. When the authorities doubted his story, Juan Diego is said to have shown them fresh roses given him by Mary despite the bleak December cold. Today, processions bearing the Virgin's image take place all over New Mexico and Arizona on December 12, with mariachi music and parishioners singing *Mañanitas,* a song for birthdays or saint's days. Pictured on the first flag carried by Mexican rebels in their revolution against Spain, the image of Our Lady of Guadalupe has become an emblem of indigenous Hispanic pride whether or not the bearer is a practicing Catholic.

HOMES

"In Our Home: Gray skies / low clouds / wet snow /
shifting wind / sandstone walls / orange light /
warm stove / scent of cedar / quiet hearts /
crackling fire / sleeping child / You and I."
— RAMSON LOMATEWAMA

Hospitality is particularly important in the Southwest during the winter season, for nights are long and the weather can be severe. With farming and most other outdoor work on hold, attention traditionally turns to keeping homes warm, stocked with food, and comfortable for the many hours to be spent indoors with family and guests.

Most Pueblo people still live in or maintain a home in a traditional village that is centuries old. Some pueblo villages are apartment-like dwellings that reflect the intimate society of Pueblo people, with shared walls built of mortared stone or mud brick roofed over with poles, brush, and adobe. Additions are made to these communities only by consensus. Pueblo villages all lie a mile or more above sea level where it is quite cold in winter, especially at night. Their snug homes are perfectly suited to this region, for in winter their stone or earthen walls absorb the low rays of the sun's warmth and their thick roofs insulate them.

Before the sixteenth century, some Pueblos were built of "puddled" adobe, which was prone to collapse. The Spanish colonists introduced adobe bricks, which were much stronger. Europeans built to last, for they were indoors much more than outside, a habit eventually adopted by Pueblo, O'odham, and even Apache and Navajo people. Many Spanish colonial homes are still standing. Their thick walls of plastered adobe or stone, supported by timbers and once roofed with tiles, are now often roofed with tin in rural areas. Centuries ago, in isolated places, homes were bunched together to present a walled perimeter as a defense against raiders, with a plaza in the center where one could work at daily tasks out of the wind. Chimayó and less well-known villages such as El Cerrito are classic examples of this design. With the church at their heart, these compact Hispanic villages are like native pueblos in that peoples' lives are interwoven socially and ceremonially. Close-knit Spanish-speaking communities persist in many Southwestern towns and cities, their perimeter walls now only metaphorical.

Founded in 1609, the city of Santa Fe was built according to the Laws of the Indies of 1572–73. These regulations directed that cities be built on a grid pattern, a Renaissance idea intended to reduce the crowding and strife of haphazard medieval towns. Albuquerque—which dates to 1706—does not conform to these principles although its founder, Francisco Cuervo y Valdéz, claimed that it did when he wrote to his superiors for approval and supplies. Only later did an official inquiry discover that he had ignored the law, and so this large old city lacks the tidy planning of the original sections of its sister to the north.

In southern Arizona, several aspects of traditional O'odham architecture endure today. Outside their little bungalows, lots of O'odham families have built cooking rooms made of brush as well as shade *ramadas,* simple, free-standing shelters where people can craft baskets or pots or relax. Often, the walls are made of ocotillo stalks planted very close together to create lovely, breezy enclosures that bloom with bright red blossoms in April. A little open space—"untended desert"—lies between dwellings in O'odham settlements now as in the past. And as they were long ago, new homes in a modern Pima development are built on berms of river cobbles which insulate them, protect them from erosion, and remind their residents of their ties to desert rivers.

Although they now live in permanent homes, traditional Apache women still teach children how to build wickiups, the light shelters once quickly assembled by their nomadic ancestors. They tell them to leave a door in the east side of their wickiup to greet the rising sun, and that they must never disturb the nest of a bird when gathering wood to build what will be, in a sense, their own nest. Special

Built of local materials in harmony with their settings, traditional homes are practical expressions of native world views. Unlike the old days, people now spend more time indoors than outside. *Clockwise from top left:* Navajo Hogan, Visitor Center, Canyon de Chelly National Monument; Governor's Office, Palace of the Governors, Santa Fe; Taos Pueblo

LUMINARIAS

"The gloom of the world is but a shadow; behind it, yet within reach, is joy. Take joy."
— FRA GIOVANNI, 1513

IN NEW MEXICO, it is the custom to light lanterns and bonfires on the longest nights of the year. On Christmas Eve, considerable stretches of the roads leading to Española, Velarde, and Truchas are lined with lighted candles inside paper sacks, while blazing stacks of piñon wood crackle in the plaza of Taos Pueblo. Southern New Mexico villages illuminate their plazas as well, and even hotels and public buildings in downtown Santa Fe and Albuquerque are ornamented with rows of electric bulbs in brown plastic bags. At one time, the lanterns were called *farolitos*—"little lamps" or "tiny beacons"—and the bonfires were known as *luminarias* (roughly, "sources of light"). Today, both the lanterns and bonfires are usually called by the latter name. In the wider world, luminarias have come to mean Christmas in New Mexico, but they do have an older, deeper significance.

Fire is symbolically important in cultures worldwide; its light often represents the good, the sacred, and the hopeful. Flames generate awe as they appear suddenly from inert material, roaring and popping and dancing like living creatures until they are extinguished. And until recently, fire was the only way to illuminate the night. It could drive away fear and darkness like the sun, lifting the spirits of those within its circle. Fire's warmth and fragrance—of burning piñon or juniper or even wax—are still a comfort on a cold, dark evening. Kindling a fire is a way to express reverence, joy, and welcome.

Southwestern people of Pueblo as well as European descent have ancient traditions of lighting fires on significant dates, especially in winter. Some Pueblos make a wintertime ceremony of igniting a flame that represents life or the return of the longed-for sun. According to Samuel Johnson's famous dictionary, to Europeans a bonfire is "a fire made for some publick cause of triumph or exaltation" (the word itself comes from the Middle Ages and means a fire of "clene" bones), hence the custom of lighting a bonfire in celebration of Christ's birth.

Many New Mexicans light rows of little lanterns to aid Mary and Joseph in their quest for shelter, or to lead the Christ child himself to their homes, perhaps in the form of relatives and other visitors. At one time, churches lit fires to guide the faithful to midnight mass, and some still have welcoming bonfires or lanterns. Luminarias were once closely identified only with New Mexico, but because they are so lovely—and perhaps because they move us in ways we hardly understand—they are now seen throughout the Southwest and in other parts of the country.

Luminarias at San Francisco de Asís, Ranchos de Taos, New Mexico

Council House of the Navajo Nation was designed to look like a huge hogan, but family hogans are quite small.

As in Apache wickiups, there is not only a specific place in a hogan for everything according to its purpose and the time it is used, but there are also rules for how to move within the hogan itself. The opening is at the east to receive the benedictions of the Dawn People who come with the sun's first rays, the south side is for storing the tools of daily life and for weaving in winter, the west side is for visiting, storytelling, and sleeping, and the north is for things used in taking care of the family including ceremonial herbs and hunting gear.

THE WINTER SOLSTICE

"The seasons, in fact, teach us two lessons that both steady and chastise: all things must pass, and all things shall return. They tell us that every new beginning brings us closer to an end, and every elegy has within it the echo (and the promise) of a future celebration."

— PICO IYER

Time seems to stand still in the depths of winter and so does the sun, for to the naked eye it appears at the same place on the dawn horizon for four days around the actual solstice date of December 21. Those who await its return encourage it with prayer, dance, and ritual, for the sun will bring with it all the good things of the coming year.

Pueblo people consider the winter solstice to be the birth of the new year and observe it with many different

wickiups or tipis are used in rites of passage and curing ceremonies.

Many Navajos build *hogans* for young brides in their families. These dwellings are sometimes prepared and blessed even when a woman and her husband do not plan to live in them, for they are a model of the orderly Navajo universe and have an important symbolic role in the couple's lives. Hogans may be built of most any material including caulked timber, stone, mud, and tar paper. Most are eight-sided and have cribbed roofs of logs laid over one another in increasingly tight circles, although one still sees an earlier form of conical hogan made of earth covering three forked logs stood on end and interlocked at the top. The modern

Artist's interpretation of elements from a Zuni altarpiece, R.B. Ravens Gallery, Ranchos de Taos, New Mexico. In the depths of winter at hearths and altars all over the Southwest, flames are lit to bring warmth to body and soul. Offerings express gratitude and recognition of life's many blessings.

customs. Prayer feathers are taken to the fields to be buried or placed on shrines. Zuni families take their prayers and wish effigies to the river and light their hearths with ceremonial firebrands upon their return. They spend an evening dancing indoors with the Shalako, who go out to make the rounds of the village the next day. Hopi hunters spend four days away from the village and bring back rabbits to stew with hominy. Katsinam arrive to bless homes and receive prayer feathers. In some places, the coming of the first katsinam was followed by a chaotic time while those emissaries went to summon others, and so spontaneity rules for a brief time in parts of Pueblo country. "Social" or non-katsina dances take place well into January, including the Harvest, Bow and Arrow, Rainbow, Turtle, and Buffalo dances, which reciprocate for blessings bestowed and demonstrate hoped-for events. Dances may be outside in the low, slanting rays of the winter sun or within churches or community buildings, sometimes at night. Some access the strength and perceptions of the animals they portray. Spectators watch the precise choreography for errors as musicians follow the drama around the plaza, keeping time for the dancers with drumbeats and song.

Performers and onlookers alike accept winter and its realities of snow, wind, and cold, for these too are essential in the cycle of life (a Southwestern saying goes: "It takes snow—not rain—to end a drought"). In the Buffalo Dance, dancers with bison headdresses surrounded by others depicting deer, pronghorns, and bighorn sheep perform a drama concerned in part with snowfall. With feather wands, Buffalo maidens pat down imaginary snow as they dance;

on their backs is a radiant image of the sun that follows a storm.

Although they reflect serious beliefs and can be very somber, there are light moments in social dances as well. Some dances imitate other groups of people. Hopis dressed as stereotypical Apaches with black page-boy wigs and skimpy breechcloths wave long-barrelled sixguns. Stout Laguna men shamble into the plaza dressed in tiered skirts like Navajo women, while real Navajo onlookers double over with good-natured laughter.

Around Christmas and on many feast days, *Matachines* perform their long, complicated, mesmerizing dances in the native pueblos and Hispanic parishes of New Mexico as well as among traditional people in southern Arizona. Accompanied by fiddle and guitar, two rows of Matachines act out pantomimes in an elaborate series of steps and turns. They wear tall hats with veils in front and capes hanging down the back, shake gourd rattles, and wave *palmas* (three-pointed wooden wands) in graceful little arabesques. Other characters play roles, too. A virginal girl in white is the mysterious figure Malinche, perhaps Cortez's translator or escort, perhaps also Montezuma's daughter or his bride. She exchanges palmas with the *monarca* or Montezuma, who lords it over everyone while at the same time being overcome himself in the course of the dance. One or more rough old masked *abuelos* (grandfathers and sometimes a grandmother) saunter and skip around cracking whips, teasing the spectators, and confronting a capering *toro* (bull). Matachines participate in religious processions also. Late in the cold, black night of Christmas Eve at Taos Pueblo,

Matachines, Indian
Pueblo Cultural Center,
Albuquerque, New Mexico.
There are as many differ-
ent interpretations of the
mysterious Matachine
dance as there are com-
munities that present it.
Scholars seek explanations
for its origins while one
generation after another
continues to perform
it. Matachine dancers
are sometimes called
"soldiers of Our Lady of
Guadalupe."

Clockwise from left: Church of San José de Gracia, Las Trampas, New Mexico; retablo (altarpiece) depicting the story of Juan Diego and Our Lady of Guadalupe, by Irene Martinez-Yates, El Rancho de las Golondrinas; bulto of San Antonio—patron saint of the poor and finder of lost articles—with the infant Jesus on his arm, Palace of the Governors, Santa Fe

they accompany an image of the Virgin Mary out of San Gerónimo Church, leading her around the plaza under showers of sparks from huge, roaring bonfires.

Matachines are classic examples of the often confused blending of traditions in the Southwest. Many believe the dance was introduced to New Mexico by Coronado himself, others say the Franciscan friars brought it, while some think it was Mexican natives accompanying Coronado who taught it to the Pueblos. As with other ancient ceremonials, its symbols may be interpreted differently according to the world-views of its practitioners. For example, the abuelos tussle with the bull during the dance and manage to castrate him. These abuelos could be just clowns or they may be ancestor spirits; the toro may be evil or he may represent the belligerent conquistadors. Parts of the dance could represent the conversion of natives to Christianity, the Spanish victory over the Moors that foreshadowed the conquest of Montezuma, or a simple allegory of good conquering evil. Certainly Spanish military and church authorities interpreted it as the latter, encouraging it and even exporting it back to the Spanish court. Recent scholars, however, suggest that it may be based on a celebration of an Aztec victory that took place not long before Cortez came to Mexico. Aztecs performed a similar dance for the Spanish, and their nobles wore the same sort of headdress. A native tradition maintains that the monarca represents a mythical figure from the south and that the dance enacts his warning to natives all over the Americas: *Strangers are coming and you will have to cooperate with them, but never relinquish your true identity.* Some people dance as Matachines in honor of a saint, but for others it is an assertion of cultural and family traditions as much as a form of prayer.

The Catholic procession of *Las Posadas* ("the lodgings") is a reenactment held just before Christmas of Joseph and Mary's search for shelter during their journey to Bethlehem. Following a couple (often a pair of children) dressed as Mary and Joseph, the procession can also include a donkey and other animals. Some participants wear shepherds' costumes (bedsheets, as often as not). The group goes from house to house singing carols and old songs, such as:

En nombre del cielo	In the name of heaven
Os pido posada	I ask of you shelter
Pues no puede andar	Since she cannot walk
Ya mi esposa amada.	Already, my beloved wife.

Those who live in the houses reply from their doorways:

Aquí no es mesón	This is not an inn
Sigan adelante	Move on, you,
Pues no puedo abrir	For I cannot open up
No sea algún tunante.	Lest it be some loafer or scoundrel.

And then shut the doors in their faces. This goes on for at least an hour if not several, for one to nine evenings depending upon the parish and its resources. Often it is cold and snowy and the procession must slither from house to house on icy streets, yet everyone sings and holds each other up until at last, they are invited into a home for refreshments. Las Posadas is a lesson in compassion during which cold and weary participants learn to appreciate the despair of those

43

who lack food or shelter. They feel in their very bones how important it is to extend hospitality to those less fortunate.

In rural Hispanic villages, there is a tradition of men dressing up as abuelos and pouncing on children at Las Posadas, demanding to know if the children can recite their prayers properly. Sometimes the children are to pray for the sick or give away their Christmas money or candy to the poor. Nowadays, the shadows of these scary abuelos still prowl the villages in the form of stories about the rewards good children receive and the troubles naughty children can bring on themselves.

Los Pastores ("The Shepherds") is a Christmas play, a jolly occasion for singing, feasting, and friendship. Tradition holds that Franciscan friars composed it based on medieval European mystery plays, as a way to teach native people about Christmas. Los Pastores took on its humorous, at times raffish character during the years of isolation from Spain. It begins with the devil and his devilish little friends hopping about in a state of rage over the coming of the Messiah. Then shepherds see a brilliant star, and an archangel of the Lord announces the birth of Christ. The shepherds set off to welcome him, dragging along their drunken friend Bartolo, who converts to a purer life when he sees the infant.

The main feast of winter for Hispanic Southwesterners is Christmas itself, usually observed on December 25 when the sun is clearly returning from its sojourn in the south. Widely celebrated in pre-Christian Europe, the winter solstice was adopted as the appropriate time to celebrate the birth of Christ, often referred to during this season as the "light of the world." From gift-giving to tamales, farolitos to family visits, a wealth of traditions surrounds the occasion.

According to Nina Otero Warren, Midnight Mass on Christmas Eve, *La Noche Buena* (the Good Night) is sometimes called *La Misa del Gallo* (the Mass of the Rooster) in the belief that it was animals in the manger who first celebrated Christ's birth. Churches are crowded with people, some of whom may not have set foot in a church any other time during the year. Though full, the churches are hushed as people kneel praying; candles burning on the altar and before images of saints are often the only sources of light. The Mass itself is long and solemn, partly sung by the priest and people, and accompanied by special music. Taking place late at night in an atmosphere of great reverence and beauty, it is an occasion when many reaffirm their faith.

The first of January is a rather arbitrary date for the beginning of the new year, being a Roman imposition to regulate the calendar rather than a date of intrinsic significance. It has become generally accepted as a secular day of celebration in the Southwest as elsewhere in the country. January 1 does fall within the cycle of winter ceremonies, and many pueblos perform dances ranging from the Matachine to the Turtle to the Apache on this date.

January 6 is another Catholic feast day known as Twelfth Night, *Epiphany* (the manifestation of divinity), or King's Day. It is a feast that emphasizes light, warmth, and peace in the home, commemorating the bright star that guided the Magi—the "three kings of Orient"—to the Christ child. Some rural Hispanic villages consider Epiphany to be the true feast of Christmas and the proper time to exchange gifts

Mission San Gerónimo,
Taos Pueblo. Originally
founded in 1617, the
mission of San Gerónimo
de Taos was destroyed
and rebuilt several times.
The present church,
which was built some
time before 1885, exem-
plifies how "European
building in New Mexico
was the creation of space
through mass and light."

in recollection of the Magi. (As Josh—narrator of Richard Bradford's classic novel of New Mexico, *Red Sky at Morning* —remarks: "Christmas on December 25 is considered a Protestant heresy in the mountains.") In some places, grand-mothers still bake a *rosca,* a ring cake with a doll inside of it, a treat which Franciscan missionaries introduced to the region perhaps four centuries ago.

King's Day is also an occasion to confirm the civil— as distinct from religious—governors of various pueblos.

In the seventeenth century, the Spanish directed each of New Mexico's Pueblos to elect civic officials by the end of each calendar year. Spanish authorities, then the Mexican government, and finally Abraham Lincoln acknowledged each pueblo's governor with an official cane with a silver head. These canes are passed on to new officials and blessed every January 6 to reaffirm order, interestingly enough right after the chaotic moon in which the solstice falls. The canes remain a potent symbol to pueblos, not

46

Some missionaries were more respectful of indigenous traditions than others were. In the 1620s, Father Fonté of Abó apparently tolerated the presence of a kiva next to the church. *Clockwise from top:* San Gregorio de Abó, Salinas Pueblo Missions National Monument; kiva mural, Kuaua Ruins, Coronado State Monument; restored great kiva, Aztec Ruins National Monument, Aztec, New Mexico

only of their governors' authority but also of trust between each tribe and the federal government. In 1987, as a protest to the inclusion of sacred Acoma lands in a new unit of the National Park System called El Malpaís, the Tribal Council of Acoma authorized their governor to take Acoma's Lincoln cane to Washington and break it.

SACRED SPACES

"In the missions of the American Southwest, the sum of the parts—Moorish and Spanish, Mestizo and Pueblo, the old world and a world older still—was and is an American architecture and interior decoration that succeeds to art of very great distinction. It is an art that reflects truly the rich cultural mosaic, the extraordinary light and colors, and above all, the sacred center of that landscape."

— N. SCOTT MOMADAY
A Sense of Mission

Pueblo people have long conducted much of their religious life within a round or square ceremonial room known as a *kiva* (plural: *kivapa*). Before ceremonies, participants spend days inside kivapa fasting, praying, smoking, and preparing the objects they will need for the ritual. Many ceremonies are private, considered appropriate only for those who have been initiated into certain societies after long and careful preparation. Among the Rio Grande pueblos, katsina dances are held in the kivapa to conceal them from the uninitiated. As Fray Silvestre Velez de Escalante reported in 1776, kivapa

are also "the chapter, or council rooms, and the Indians meet in them, sometimes to discuss matters of their government for the coming year, their planting, arrangements for work to be done, or to elect new community officials, or to rehearse their dances, or sometimes for other things." Kivapa evolved from very ancient pre-Puebloan dwellings that were dug into the ground. During the classical Pueblo period around the twelfth century, some of these chambers were huge, big enough for hundreds of people. The layout of today's pueblos, with their dance plazas surrounded by dwellings whose roofs serve as a vantage point for spectators, may have evolved from those "Great Kivas."

To Apaches, the tipi used in ceremonies to observe the landmarks in life—such as birth, first steps, and the onset of a girl's puberty—is a model of the universe. Its opening is to the east, the direction of life, while death lies closed off to the west. Among the White Mountain Apaches, ceremonial tipis are supported by a pole of piñon pine in the east, walnut to the south, one of juniper for the west, and gambel oak on the north side, as symbols of the four directions. Navajo hogans are likewise cosmic models and many ceremonies, including marriage, take place in them. Other rituals are set out of doors or in sweat lodges.

A few O'odham villages have traditional *rainhouses,* or *roundhouses,* in which men make village decisions and carry out ceremonies. Like Pueblo kivas, roundhouses are good examples of architectural continuity from their culture's early days. They are made in the old way with brush walls and a dry earth roof, for to use mud mortar would be a sacrilegious waste in such arid country. There is nothing

elaborate about roundhouses; the spiritual creativity of
the original O'odham religion is poured into songs, stories,
dances, and pilgrimages.

Even after the Spanish no longer sent priests to
minister to them, the Tohono O'odham grafted Catholic
teachings onto their original beliefs in a unique way.
According to folklorist Jim Griffith, the *Jios himdag* (God
Way) or *santo himdag* (Saint Way) "appears for the most
part to be based on kinds of observable Catholic ritual
behavior that have been integrated into what is basically
an O'odham system for preserving balance and health in
families and communities." The Tohono O'odham built
simple folk chapels with three-sided ramadas and dance
grounds next to them, where they still conduct an ever-
evolving mix of ceremonies.

The Catholic churches of New Mexico and Arizona are
conspicuous examples of the *syncretism*—the reconciliation
of diverse practices—attempted between the original and
the introduced cultures of the Southwest. With their arched
ceilings supported by columns, European churches once
emulated the sacred groves of trees where their ancestors
worshipped. Already a blend of European and North
African elements, Spanish sacred architecture adapted to
new settings in the Southwest, in part because native artisans
did most of the work and used local materials. Surrounding
landforms also influenced sacred architecture to the point
where some churches—San José at Laguna, for example—
echo the shapes of their setting. In addition, at least one
church—San Gregorio de Abó—had an active kiva in its
courtyard, at least for a time.

ICONOGRAPHY

"Then weave for us a garment of brightness;
    May the warp be the white light of morning,
    May the weft be the red light of evening,
    May the fringes be the falling rain,
    May the border be the standing rainbow."
    — THE SONG OF THE SKY LOOM *(Tewa)*

As may be seen at Kuaua Pueblo, kiva walls traditionally
bear murals that are ritually renewed or replaced often.
Brightly colored geometric patterns like those of textiles or
pottery, abstract feathers and clouds, frogs and fish, flowers
and corn, and warriors and supernatural beings cover the
walls. Some scholars consider it incorrect to refer to these
murals as "art," because the meaning and purpose of these
pictures is sacred and the local native languages have no
words corresponding to "art." However, holy pictures fill art
museums all over the world and elements of kiva murals
form the basis for much of Pueblo fine art today.

During Pueblo dances and other ceremonies, katsinam
give little girls *tithu,* or flat katsina dolls carved from cottonwood roots. Although these dolls represent sacred beings,
they are meant to be played with, for becoming knowledge-
able about these beings is vital. Each katsina has a wealth
of characteristics that distinguish it from others, especially
the designs on its face and body and the things it carries.
Dolls carved for sale may be very abstract, but their identities
are still recognizable by their colors and specific features.
Animate katsinam also move in a particular way and make

Sacred imagery takes many forms in the Southwest, sometimes portraying a realm beyond everyday reality, and often the enduring presence and concern of holy beings. *Clockwise from left:* Petroglyphs, Saguaro National Monument, Arizona; Navajo sandpainting and Hopi morning katsina, both from Broken Arrow Gallery, Taos, New Mexico

distinctive sounds. Even so, change is ongoing. Katsinam added since the coming of Europeans include the cow and the chicken.

Sand paintings—which may also be made of colored cornmeal and pollen—are a more ephemeral element of Pueblo ceremonials. At some point, Navajo *hataałii* adapted them to depict the activities of the Holy People. Sand paintings used in ceremonies are swept away afterwards, but in recent years certain designs from these paintings have been woven into Navajo rugs or fixed onto thin boards with glue to be sold to non-natives.

All over the region, there are petroglyphs (pecked images) and pictographs (paintings) on stone. Some of these have been dated to the Archaic period several thousand years before agriculture was introduced. Many apparently represent the shamanistic side of Southwestern cultures, depicting journeys taken or phenomena encountered in dreams and trances. Natural holes in the rock may be enhanced or incorporated into the pictures. (Apache shamans consider stones to be where certain spirits reside.) Petroglyphs may show a shaman on a heroic quest about to enter a passage to another world, suffering, or even dying to be reborn with knowledge of that "other world." Birds and other animals appear to be singing or speaking with scroll-work coming out of their open mouths. Ancient stories tell us that cranes guard Pueblo katsinam and are cherished spirit helpers of the O'odham. Human figures often hold canes, symbols of power that are virtually universal. There are also "phosphenes," entoptic images (produced by the optic nerve) that humans see when in altered states of consciousness.

Altered states, sought by self-selected members of all of the cultures in this book, may be induced by hallucinogens but also by fasting, sleep-deprivation, or another means of "mortifying the flesh." Many rock art sites have obviously been revisited for centuries including our own; images have been added or renewed as if these are indeed sites of vision quests and shamanistic apprenticeships. There are other ways to explain rock art: Dr. Jane Young perceives a close relationship between Zuni petroglyphs and sacred poetry.

Catholics also believe that symbolic imagery can illuminate the path to the divine and their older churches in particular are often richly decorated. From the earliest days, artisans carved and painted European or "Moorish" designs and images in churches but sometimes also depicted the revered and familiar elements of the local people: flowers, corn, rainbows, and birds. At first, most of the statuary for churches came from Mexico or even Spain. If locally made, it was usually copied from expertly carved, imported figures. However, as Spanish wealth and influence waned in New Mexico and Arizona, it became necessary for people to do the best they could when adding to or replacing the images of saints in their churches. Local artisans began to paint simple scenes on planks of wood to serve as *reredos,* or altar screens. They carved figures of saints, called *bultos*, from gypsum, cottonwood root, or pine. *Santeros* painted *santos,* or saints, on either animal hides (to the horror of the occasional visiting authority) or on wood. Collectors value these icons for the earnest simplicity with which they are made, but they are sincerely venerated in Hispanic and Pueblo communities, placed within churches and homes, carried

Retablo by *santero* Rafael Aragón, depicting the Virgin of Sorrows, a crowned Saint Joseph with the infant Jesus, and Saint Lawrence, Church of Santa Cruz de la Cañada, Santa Cruz, New Mexico. "Saints...share in the living tradition of prayer by the example of their lives, the transmission of their writings, and their prayer today."
— *The Catechism*

in processions, and sometimes put on a table outside for special occasions—to oversee a Matachine or a Corn dance, for example.

Among the austere figures of robed priests, nuns, and other saints from the Bible that are found in Southwestern Catholic churches, there is usually an incongruous statue of El Santo Niño de Atocha, a chubby boy dressed in lace, a velvet cloak, and a flouncy hat. The child is credited with a host of miracles, beginning with the days when the Moors still held Spain and were believed to have wrongfully imprisoned many Christian men. At Atocha outside Madrid, these prisoners could have no visitors except the children who brought them food, one of whom—El Santo Niño—carried a miraculous basket of bread and flask of water that were never empty. As a representation of the child Jesus who made many journeys himself, he is a protector of travelers. El Santo Niño holds a special place in the hearts of Hispanic Southwesterners, for travel in colonial days was often necessary but extremely hazardous.

Expeditions of the Spanish Empire were required to produce accounts of the people and customs they encountered in the Americas. Native artists illustrated a number of these accounts with paintings of native ceremonies, as in Diego Durán's *Historia de las Indias de Nueva España* and Juan de Tovar's *Relación de los Indios*. Southwest artists from all backgrounds continue to paint pictures of ceremonials, now as fine art available for purchase. But in a sense, these paintings still fulfill at least part of the same purpose as ancient rock art and kiva murals: they illustrate a certain way of regarding the divine. And the cross-fertilization continues: murals in the Catholic church at Zuni depict katsinam, and *Ga an* dance around the figure of Christ behind the altar at Saint Francis Catholic Church in Whiteriver, Fort Apache, Arizona.

Brittlebush and saguaros, Saguaro National Monument, and Mariachis, La Mesilla, New Mexico

S P R I N G

SPRING

Cholla cactus in bloom,
Pecos National Monument,
New Mexico

SPRING APPROACHES THE SOUTHWEST LIKE AN ENERGETIC BUT BASHFUL CHILD—DASHING IN THEN BACKING AWAY, HIDING AND THEN SHYLY APPROACHING AGAIN. EVEN THE QUALITY OF LIGHT FLICKERS BACK AND FORTH, FROM FEEBLE SHAFTS OF THE WINTER SUN TO THE BROAD, GOLDEN BEAMS OF SUMMER. BUT HERE AND there, bright blossoms of red paintbrush emerge even where snow still patches the north country. Filaree—a tiny, magenta geranium introduced very early from the Mediterranean— pops up too, in sunny spots all across the Southwest. Spring is a time of renewal; days grow longer and warmer and every- one delights in each new leaf that emerges. One of the great joys of spring is when colorful birds return to the higher regions: violet-green swallows, red-breasted robins, and their powder-blue cousins, the mountain bluebirds. Flickers call urgently from treetops and mourning doves coo from thickets. Even the ominous turkey vulture is welcomed back, an agent of purification to clear away winter-killed carrion.

The season's progress is the opposite of orderly. The only predictable thing about spring is that it will be windy, with flashes of pollen glinting in the air on its way to fertilize grasses, sagebrush, and pine. There are years when spring rains tear apart the delicate brush weirs O'odham farmers make to distribute water across their fields. Then the southern deserts are carpeted with wildflowers, and the sharp fragrance of rain-drenched creosotebush bursts upon the senses. In other years, weeks of waiting and supplication yield no rain at all or if rain does come, bursts of it may soak one family's field while puffs of dust whirl across the neighbor's. In the north, streams can rise to spill over their banks or remain mere trickles; arroyos may channel torrents of snow-melt or stay bone-dry gullies. Tall pines stand dark and mysterious in soft patters of rain or roar like an ocean in surges of desiccating winds.

EMERGING FROM DARKNESS

"For seasons release us from time and space, and usher us into an order higher than ourselves, or nation, or ideology; not so much a collective religion, perhaps, as a religion of collectivism. And seasons rescue us from private winters and admit us to a larger rhythm as unanswerable as the dawn."

— PICO IYER

Solar calendars mark the beginning of spring on February 2, as the sun brings increasing hours of warmth and daylight. This cross-quarter day—midway between the winter solstice and the spring equinox—is celebrated across the United States as Ground Hog Day, when the forecast for the season is still "up in the air." To enhance their strength and virtue for successful farming and coax along beneficial weather, Pueblo, O'odham, and Hispanic farmers shed winter during a period of fasting and ritual beginning around this time, readying both body and spirit for the hard work of longer days.

Among the Hopi, it is the end of the winter social dance season and time for *Powamuya* or the Bean Dance, when the katsinam come to the villages to stay. Many different katsinam appear, each strolling or dancing, whirling or

running, hooting, calling, or remaining mute according to its nature. They proceed through the villages—sometimes in a snowstorm, sometimes in sunshine—reestablishing their presence among the people and giving wonderful things to children. The customs of each village are different; infants may receive simple, flat katsina dolls *(tithu),* colorful plaques, lightning sticks, or ceremonial shoes, while the katsinam might give older girls more elaborate katsina dolls,

55

Áholi katsina, Museum of Northern Arizona. "We do not perceive the katsina dolls simply as carved figurines or brightly decorated objects. They have important meaning to us, the Hopi people: We believe they are personifications of the katsina spirits, originally created by the katsinam in their physical embodiment." — Alph Secakuku

basketry, plaques, dancing wands, or shoes. Boys may be given bows and arrows, lightning sticks, or moccasins. The katsinam also pass around humming toys, tops, and rattles so that the children may make sounds like the wind that brings the rain. Frightening ogres with bulging eyes and beaklike, toothed mouths stomp around ensuring that the village is maintaining high moral standards. Whipper katsinam may flick people with yucca lashes to correct or discipline them; others afflicted with certain illnesses request lashings that will strengthen them. Runner katsinam are sent off with prayers for rain, and households receive bundles of foot-long bean sprouts to simmer in a traditional stew.

February 2 is one of numerous occasions when the ancient calendars of the New Mexico Pueblos coincide with the Catholic year. Pueblos hold dances and native and Hispanic Catholics attend special masses for *Candelaria,* or Candlemas Day. Once called the Feast of the Purification after an ancient Jewish rite for new mothers, it is now celebrated as the Feast of the Presentation of the Lord, which commemorates Christ's appearance in the temple in Jerusalem. Priests bless the candles that will illuminate churches all through the coming year, and in farming villages they also bless seeds that will soon be planted in the fields.

On Ash Wednesday in February (the exact date depends upon the phases of the moon), Catholics attend Mass and receive ashes on their foreheads as a sign of penance for past transgressions and as a reminder to "remember you are dust and to dust you shall return." Lent, a time of preparation for Easter, begins four days later. For the forty days of Lent (if counted from Ash Wednesday to

Easter, as many Catholics do), many Catholics attend Mass every day, abstain from certain foods and drink, give alms, and dedicate themselves to a regimen of prayer and good works. Hispanic churches resonate daily with the voices of devout men's and women's societies singing long prayers, alternating verses from one side of the church to the other, often for hours.

Apaches and Navajos generally divide the year into winter and summer. The conjunction of constellations called Thunder and Bear—in the lunar month corresponding to March—marks when hibernating animals and dormant plants are aroused from their sleep by the "white" thunder prefiguring the beginning of summer.

THE FOUR DIRECTIONS

"Praised be my Lord for our brother the wind, and for air and cloud, calms and all weather, by which thou upholdest in life all creatures."

— SAINT FRANCIS OF ASSISI
Canticle of the Sun

In a region where one can see often a hundred miles in any direction, it is clear where snow, rain, and light itself originate. Winter storm fronts tend to come from the Pacific to the north and west, while summer's thunderheads boil up as moist air invades the desert mainly from the south and east. The point on the horizon where the sun rises and sets moves north to south and back again across the seasons. After watching these phenomena for centuries, the native people

Box Canyon Ruin with the snowy San Francisco Peaks in the background, Wupatki National Monument, Arizona. Over eight centuries old, Wupatki's many ruins are a reminder of the long and intimate bond between this landscape and its native people, to whom the distant peaks remain sacred.

of the Southwest ascribe qualities to the four directions, associate them with certain powers, animals, and colors, and call to those directions for blessings. In addition, each direction has both a mythological and a remembered history. Stories tell of culture heroes journeying to or from these directions and of migrational paths to present homelands.

Symbolic and spiritual geography varies from pueblo to pueblo. While Hopi, Zuni, Jemez, and the Keresan pueblos regard north as the direction of yellow, west as blue, south as red, and east as white, Picurís associates north with black, west with yellow, south with blue, and east with white. Some define the cardinal directions by the farthest points on the horizon where the sun rises and sets, i.e., northeast, southeast, southwest, and northwest. Except for the Tiwa, Pueblos define two other directions as well: "up" or the zenith, and the nadir. In addition to associating the four directions with certain birds, most of the pueblos connect the east with the wolf, the west with the bear, and the north with the mountain lion, but south may be associated with the wildcat or, among the Zuni and Tewa, the badger.

Man-in-the-Maze patterned Tohono O'odham basket, Museum of Northern Arizona. "Bridging the gulf between . . . cultures is exceedingly difficult since it involves moving from one universe of experience through a set of mutually confusing concepts to the reality of the other culture."
—Vine Deloria, Jr.

A proper Apache or Navajo awakens before dawn and prays with the sun rising in the east. To Apaches, the east is "where the sun comes up" and therefore a realm of beginnings and the source of the life force. Everything was black before the beginning of the world, and so east is symbolized by the color black. South is "the direction of midday" where the rain people come from, and its color ranges from blue to turquoise to green. West is "where the sun sets;" its color may be yellow or red. North is "the direction of the Big Dipper" and is white for purification, as it is where Yusin greets those who have left this earth.

Navajos associate the east with dawn, light, fire, white shell, and the color white, and with physical and mental awareness; the south with the earth, work, responsibility, turquoise stone, and the color blue; the west with water, abalone shell, twilight, the color yellow, and social responsibility; the north with air, night, coal, the color black, and ceremonies. To each of these directions there is also ascribed a Holy Wind. Navajos consider air—whether in motion or not—to be Holy Wind, believing that it suffuses all beings with life, thought, speech, and the power to move. In Navajo ceremonials, the final act is to breathe in the air at dawn to restore the indwelling presence of the supreme Holy Wind.

Perhaps it is this emphasis on the sky and the cardinal directions that has led native cultures of the Southwest to see four parts to things in general. Four winds blow, and there are four stages of life. Pictures of the sun, moon, and stars have four points; four lines are painted on roof beams for strength. Each New Mexico pueblo reveres four nearby

peaks, while four primary sacred mountains enclose the *Dinetah*—land of the Navajo—and four *Ga an* uphold the Apache universe. Acts of reverence are performed four times, four offerings are made on altars, and so on.

The Blessing of Water

"Praised be my Lord for our sister water, who is very serviceable unto us, and humble, and precious, and clean. Praised be my Lord for our mother the earth, that which doth sustain us and keep us, and bringeth forth diverse fruits, and flowers of many colors, and grass."

— Saint Francis of Assisi
Canticle of the Sun

With the spring equinox on about March 21, days finally begin to grow longer than nights. It is time for farmers to begin the work of preparing the fields that will feed their families. Spring is an optimistic time for traditional Southwestern farmers whether they are Pueblo or O'odham, Apache, Navajo, or Hispanic. Each visits his field with offerings and prayers to assess what needs to be done before planting. In the dry climates of New Mexico and Arizona, the most critical task is to make the most of every drop of snowmelt or rainfall.

Southwestern farmers have long practiced sustainable agriculture. With small-scale but intensive systems of check-dams, brush walls, catchment basins, and ditches patiently developed over centuries, they channel water from washes and streams to irrigate their fields. Tohono O'odham farmers can harvest remarkable yields of beans, corn, and even watermelons without any source of water other than as little as three to five inches of rain, in a region where daytime temperatures may top one hundred degrees for more than half the year. They plant seeds that are the result of centuries of selection of drought-tolerant types, in combinations that invite beneficial insects in to prey upon other insects who could destroy the harvest. By distributing the runoff that floods down desert washes across their fields during the infrequent rainstorms, O'odham farmers actually add to the fertility of their fields. Flood debris—animal droppings, leaf litter, and twigs—acts as a mulch rich in nitrogen and other nutrients. There are only a few Tohono O'odham farmers who use the old methods on a hundred or so acres now, although ten thousand acres were farmed in this way around the turn of the century. But as so often happens in human history, the old ways are being reexamined just on the brink of extinction, as groundwater is depleted and other aspects of modern desert agriculture are found to be neither cost-effective nor good for the land.

Hopis are "dry farmers" also. Hopi mesas and fields receive as little as five to seven inches of rain annually and are higher in elevation than those of the O'odham. The growing season is short and so plants must be vigorous to ripen between frosts. Ancient methods still bring success here too, to an extent that is so astonishing it is little wonder that farming is a sacred pursuit revered by Hopi communities. Ethnobotanist Gary Paul Nabhan tells this delightful story:

We took a lot of seed up to the Hopi. We distributed it to over a hundred families; we offered a special prize at the Hopi Fair—a set of garden tools to the person the Hopi people themselves felt was maintaining the old crops best. This year they split the prize between a nine-year-old boy and a seventy-year-old man.

In addition to controlling floodwater, the O'odham and some eastern Pueblos have created systems of canals. Small-scale canals were a vital part of the civilization of southern Arizona's early people, who today are called by the O'odham name of *Hohokam* ("vanished" or "all used up"). Vestiges of their irrigation canals can be seen in many places, including the Hohokam ruins at Pueblo Grande in Phoenix and at Casa Grande. Such hand-dug watercourses appear even far to the north, near ruined settlements in places that were influenced by Hohokam traders such as Montezuma Well. The O'odham continued to use some of these aqueducts after the demise of Hohokam civilization (which some scholars believe was caused by floods that devastated their canals). When Spanish settlers came to southern Arizona, they enhanced and added to the ancient irrigation ditches. Canals led from missions through kitchen gardens to fields, which, according to folklorist Jim Griffith, explains the layout of streets in old parts of Tucson. Anglo settlement of the Phoenix area was hastened in large part because of existing canals. In fact, this resurrection of a thriving agricultural community along the arteries of an ancient one gave the new city its unusual name.

Scarce and undependable, water is precious for it brings life to the domesti-cated and the wild alike. *Clockwise from left:* Rio Grande below Taos; corn petroglyph, Village of the Great Kivas, Zuni Nation, New Mexico; blooming prickly pear cactus, Tumacácori National Historical Park, Arizona

Anthropologist Edward Dozier believes that irrigation canals were the main reason for the religious and social differences between the eastern Pueblos along the Rio Grande and the western Pueblos of Zuni, Acoma, Laguna, and especially Hopi. According to this view, eastern Pueblos take a practical rather than religious approach to farming because irrigation affords them considerable control over the outcome. The organization of eastern villages evolved into large societies, or *sodalities,* probably in order to maintain ditch systems. Dozier points out that western Pueblos take a more mystical approach to their lives as farmers and have arranged their society in terms of small clans that have ceremonial functions rather than labor-related roles in the community.

One of the main differences between the extensive Spanish colonization of New Mexico and their limited incursion into Arizona was the availability of water for irrigation. The Rio Grande is an easily reached, life-sustaining corridor with many tributaries. It runs the length of New Mexico from north to south. In southern Arizona, the San Pedro and Santa Cruz Rivers provide much smaller avenues, and only about as far as Tucson. Northern Arizona has no north-south river to support either conquest or irrigated agriculture. Europeans seldom ventured very far north in Arizona until after the American Civil War.

When Spanish settlers arrived in New Mexico, local people say that one of the first things they did was dig an irrigation ditch near Santa Cruz. They added European and North African irrigation techniques and devices to the Pueblo custom of diverting water into their fields from nearby streams. Today, there are ditches on every stream system in New Mexico, about eight hundred in all. They are the oldest public works system in the state, a continuation of the canals dug by ancestors of today's Pueblos. Called by their Arabic name *acequias,* these ditches distribute water from the Rio Grande, Pecos, and their tributaries to thousands of small farmers, forming the economic base of Pueblo and Hispanic communities throughout the region.

The Pueblo and Hispanic people who depend upon acequias participate in one of the oldest forms of government in the Southwest, a very pure form of democracy. In spring, acequia *parciantes*—sharers of the water from a ditch system—meet with their *mayordomos,* or nominal leaders. They discuss the condition of the acequias, their individual needs, and the quantity of water likely to be available that year from snowmelt and rain. Frictions are resolved and the water is apportioned. The work necessary to prepare the acequia is apportioned as well, for acequias are a community effort.

Soon afterwards—in some villages around the spring equinox—the parciantes meet at the ditch itself, armed with shovels, picks, hoes, and axes. All along its length, they clear out debris that has accumulated since harvest time. It is hard but happy work, a time of hope, dreams, and reunion, for sons who live as far away as Los Angeles and Chicago return to help their fathers. Birds sing in the cottonwoods lining the acequias and shoots of new green life appear everywhere. Priests lead processions to bless the ditches. As in native religions, water signifies great blessings in the Catholic faith. The sixteenth-century Saint Teresa of Ávila compared the many ways of watering a garden—which range from the

CINCO DE MAYO

"Cinco de Mayo can and should be celebrated by everyone who believes in and supports the right of every country to be free, the struggles for social justice around the world, and the right of every individual to struggle against unjust conditions and institutions."

— DR. ALMA GARCIA
Santa Clara University

EVERY YEAR, Mexican Americans across the Southwest hold parades and parties on *Cinco de Mayo*, the fifth of May. This is probably the Southwest's most important nonreligious event for people of Mexican descent, a happy celebration that is lively with brightly costumed *folklorico* (folk) dancing, spirited mariachi music, and traditional spicy foods. Although Cinco de Mayo is widely assumed to commemorate Mexico's independence from Spain, it does not—the Mexican declaration of Independence is celebrated on September 16. The real story of Cinco de Mayo dates to 1862, more than forty years after the end of Spanish rule.

In 1821, three centuries after the arrival of the conquistador Hernán Cortes in 1519, Mexico won its independence from Spain. The country remained unstable for decades, however, due to clashes between the Conservatives, largely descendants of European colonists who had prospered under Spanish rule, and the Liberals, mostly indigenous and *mestizo* (mixed ancestry) Mexicans who envisioned a country of equal opportunity for all. In addition, a long fight to prevent encroachment by its northern neighbor bankrupted Mexico and led to the demoralizing loss of Texas in 1836 and nearly half its remaining

Cinco de Mayo, La Mesilla, New Mexico

territory to the United States in 1848 (including those lands that became the states of Arizona and New Mexico).

Conservative elements in Mexico appealed to European leaders to restore the stability once imposed by the Spanish colonial administration, but those distant powers hesitated. President Benito Juarez, a Zapotec Indian from Oaxaca, suspended the payment of Mexico's foreign debts for two years, and only then did the leaders of Spain, England, and France send

troops to Mexico to restore the old social and economic order and force repayment of their loans. Although the other powers soon withdrew, Napoléon III of France persisted.

Napoléon's troops advanced quickly across Mexico but on May 5, 1862, they were defeated by a relatively small and ill-equipped force of Mexican loyalists, or Liberals, at the Battle of Puebla. This was a short-lived victory for the Liberals for by 1864, the Emperor Maximilian (an Austrian Hapsburg) ruled Mexico with the support of Napoléon's troops. The Liberals were badly outgunned, but they continued to wage a guerrilla war against the French soldiers. Napoléon eventually withdrew his troops from what had become an expensive quagmire, Juarez again became president, and the hapless Emperor Maximilian was executed. However, Mexico was so weakened and impoverished that in some respects it has still not recovered.

Because it was the poor, the idealistic, and the indigenous who defeated well-supplied, professional European soldiers at the Battle of Puebla on the fifth of May, that event is a symbol of the struggle by common people for economic, social, and racial justice and pride. For those of Mexican descent who live in areas of the United States that were once part of Mexico, there is an added fervor in the celebration of this holiday, which is celebrated with more fanfare here than in Mexico itself. Cinco de Mayo celebrates an idealized Mexico, the country that might have been born if only its people had been supported in their efforts to forge a new nation.

Acequia-irrigated fields below Villanueva, New Mexico. The skilled channeling of water broadens the ribbon of life flourishing on the edges of streams in New Mexico. Techniques developed by north Africans—added to those of the indigenous people of the American Southwest—have created oases along the Pecos River as well as along the Rio Grande and its tributaries.

deliberate work of maintaining acequias to the passively grateful acceptance of rain—to the different forms of prayer.

Later, farmers work alone again as they open the gates from the acequias into their fields. In late springtime, it is not unusual to come upon a lone figure standing in a sunlit field, singing as the shining water flows into furrows he has planted with chiles, beans, and sweet corn.

Ironically, the poorest people in New Mexico possess its most valuable resource: water. Existing water rights take precedence over all other developments proposed for the state. There is considerable pressure on Pueblos as well as Hispanic parciantes to give up their water to developers in exchange for cash but most resist, feeling that to do so would be to sell their children's cultural and economic legacy.

Property

> "The Spaniards did recognize the rights of the Pueblos
> to the lands upon which they were living. . . . Land
> grants by the Spaniards did serve to help preserve
> the Pueblo Indian culture and religion, to an extent
> greater than that allowed by other European powers."
> — Joe S. Sando
> Jemez educator

Pueblo and O'odham communities assigned the land itself to families by a combination of tradition and consensus. When Spanish administrators returned to New Mexico after the Pueblo Revolt, they recognized the villages and traditional farming lands of the Pueblo people (although not their hunting, gathering, or ceremonial territories). However presumptuous it may seem to us now, the crown conferred land grants on each Pueblo community and, later, on the O'odham in southern Arizona. Incoming colonists honored these grants for the most part, since the Spanish authorities granted them separate land. Rather than parceling out all of their land grants among individuals, many native and Hispanic villages maintained *ejidos,* or areas of land held in common for grazing, water, and wood. There followed a time of relatively peaceful coexistence in which native and Hispanic neighbors exchanged seeds, livestock, and expertise. But as the Spanish population increased, the populations of Pueblos and O'odham fell, mostly as a result of introduced diseases. Some settlers violated the native grants, usually by grazing their cattle on unused land but sometimes

by actually moving there themselves. Although the Spanish governors were assiduous record-keepers, these violations were not always prosecuted and so the boundaries of the original grants became blurred.

An effort to convert the Apaches to farming on reservations called *establecimientos de paz* ("establishments of peace") was not successful for a variety of reasons. Apaches were culturally still nomadic people, well armed and mounted by the 1700s. After centuries of tangling with the Spanish and other settled people, they had become accustomed to raiding rather than farming. Although the Navajo *were* farmers, neither they nor the Apache were deeded lands in perpetuity by the Spanish.

The 1848 Treaty of Guadalupe Hidalgo, in which Mexico ceded New Mexico and Arizona to the United States, guaranteed the continuation of the original Spanish land grants. Early American settlers rarely respected these grants, however. Later, the Dawes Act of 1887 created pressure on native people to sell their land. More recently, however, legislation such as the Pueblo Lands Act of 1924 established a legal process by which grants may be resecured and in some cases, expanded. The Spanish land grant is very much alive today, with litigation pending on behalf of many native and Hispanic claimants. In addition, indigenous people are asserting their rights (admittedly with mixed results) on the basis that, as Governor Paytiamo of Acoma put it: "Federal and state laws may take away our lands under newly instituted laws but our people remain intact with the land. As our Acoma elders say, 'We are already underneath the land.'" In 1970, the sacred Blue Lake of

66

Corn Mountain, Zuni
Nation, New Mexico.
"A holy place can adopt
distinct forms; it can
be a grove of trees, a
spring, a mountain, or
sometimes a city or a
temple where relics are
venerated; it is a visible
sign of the contact
between the human and
the divine." —Pilgrims'
Museum, Santiago de
Compostela, Spain

Taos was returned to that Pueblo by the Carson National Forest—the first native land to be legally recovered from the U.S. government for religious reasons.

SHRINES AND PILGRIMAGES

"The foreign country somehow gets under the skin of those born in it. Certain very primitive tribes are convinced that it is not possible to usurp foreign territory, because the children born there would inherit the wrong ancestor-spirits who dwell in the trees, the rocks, and the water of that country."
— CARL GUSTAV JUNG
Civilization in Transition

Shrines are physical manifestations of metaphysical powers, places to direct one's prayers, offerings, and gratitude. Southwestern cultures regard all of the earth as sacred, yet also revere countless shrines in particular places that hold exceptional significance. Sometimes these places are where a mythical or historical event occurred, or where a certain power is believed to reside. They may be homes for spirits or niches for saints, placed where their presence is most needed and believers may seek their help. There are travelers' shrines along ancient pathways, sacred caves in the flanks of mountains, and holy springs of life-sustaining water. Many Hispanics set aside a corner of their modest homes for a small shrine where they offer daily prayers. Farmers build and make offerings to shrines beside their fields, and individuals seeking visions undertake arduous journeys to

distant peaks, lakes, and canyons. Every village has shrines, whether to the four directions or to its patron saint or to both, where gifts are presented during ceremonies and feast days.

In some places, there may be a series of shrines where Pueblo people offer prayers to establish a pathway for rain clouds to follow to their village. Certain Pueblos also believe that there are underground passages connecting their villages or nearby shrines and their sacred mountains—Black Mesa and the hill of Tsi Mayoh for which the village of Chimayó is named, for instance. According to local writer Don Usner, legend relates that people tested this passageway long ago. They built a fire at one end, and smoke came out the other! Pueblo people offer gifts at such caves and passageways for the spirits that inhabit them.

There are two very famous shrines in O'odham country, although they are by no means the only ones there. The first is a cave on Baboquivari Mountain that is believed to be the home of I'itoi. Offerings left here range from rosaries and saints' medallions to jars of cactus syrup. The second is the Children's Shrine, which lies next to a desert wash. Long ago, a hunter tried to kill a badger there, a very wrongful act indeed. A flood gushed forth, threatening to inundate all of O'odham country. The people learned that they must give what they most cherished to stop it. Four of their beloved children were swallowed by water. Their relatives placed ocotillo stalks there at the points of the four directions. Villagers renew these stalks every fourth spring, for to fail in this would be to risk the failure of the crops. It seems the children are alive and have an influence over what happens nearby.

Rock formations, Chiricahua
National Monument,
Arizona. Three related
bands of Apaches—who
foraged across the rugged
landscape of what is now
southern New Mexico and
Arizona—became known
as the *Chiricahua* after
this highland maze. This
cool "sky island," which
sustains a great diversity of
plants and animals, was
home to the Chokona band
of Chiricahua Apaches.

Pilgrims undertake devotional journeys all over New Mexico and Arizona, passing as if invisible through business districts and national parks, crossing over remote mountain ranges and even across national boundaries into Mexico. Pueblo people still make pilgrimages to shrines located within ancient ruins, such as the lion shrine at Bandelier National Monument in New Mexico. Each August, the people of Taos make a pilgrimage into the mountains high above them to visit Blue Lake, source of the pueblo's river.

It is said that some O'odham still leave offerings such as tobacco at the shrines of departed shamans and ancestors and at the slowly dissolving adobe ruins of the long-vanished Hohokam. In the O'odham ceremonial cycle, there are other pilgrimages appropriate for each season of the year. Individuals undertake these journeys to obtain objects which must be blessed (and the pilgrim himself purified) before they enter the village, for their presence is considered very powerful. At one time, O'odham men obtained power for curing by slaying an enemy or trapping and plucking the feathers of an eagle, or by traveling south for salt from the Gulf of California.

The salt pilgrimage is certainly one of the most remarkable traditional journeys in the Southwest, taking about four days on horseback across hot, barren, almost waterless desert. Even at waterholes, the men must only drink a little bit, as the trip is a deliberate ordeal intended to induce visions of spirit guides. When they reach the northern end of the Sea of Cortez, which has some of the highest tides in the world (more than forty-three feet on

some occasions), the men are to collect kernels of salt that resemble and are called "corn," and give cornmeal to the ocean in return for the salt. Some may swim out into the sea, an almost unimaginable sensation for desert dwellers. A period of purification will be necessary upon their return to their villages, for they have been in contact with a source of great power. No one is known to have made the salt pilgrimage for the past forty or fifty years, but with the resurgence of cultural identity among the O'odham, it may again take place soon.

For an Apache diyi (medicine man) to obtain power, he or she must take a dream-journey, a vision-quest to a holy place. Such places are often in the mountains where a spirit being, animal, or plant may take human form to explain the intent of ceremonies. Later, the person must learn the details of how to conduct those rituals from another person who practices them, but it is the journey that puts the pilgrim in touch with the actual source of the power. Apaches also make reverent pilgrimages to mountain shrines simply to pray, alone or with others.

Among traditional Navajo, it is appropriate to make a pilgrimage to one or more of the sacred mountains every summer, for a *Blessingway* ceremony in which a Navajo hataałii sings of the journeys and triumphs of the Holy People and Warrior twins in order to restore hózhǫ́, the state of harmony. Some Apache and Navajo people carry corn pollen at all times in order to offer it at the sacred sites they may pass. To lead a correct life is described in the Navajo language as "following the pollen path," or "following the path of dew" as in this song:

Left, from top: Roadside shrine, Tohono O'odham Nation; roadside shrine near Chimayó, New Mexico; folk shrine of El Tiradito, "the little fellow cast (or shot) away," Tucson. Nobody knows which version of El Tiradito's sudden demise— whether as innocent bystander, robbery victim, or member of a lovers' triangle—is the original story. *Right:* El Santuario de Chimayó

SPRING

May I walk in harmony.
May we live in harmony.
May we communicate in harmony.
May I walk in the path of dew.

It is often said that native people revere the earth in a way that Europeans do not, but that generalization is probably based on the relatively recent history of this country. In Europe, the countryside is dotted with shrines where local people still leave flowers and other gifts for the saints and sometimes the pre-Christian spirits of those places. Holy wells, sacred hills, and hallowed groves of trees are found all over rural Spain, Italy, France, and Britain, among other countries. The Spanish people who settled New Mexico came from this tradition, and soon perceived the numinous in the natural world all around them here as well. In some cases they adopted local beliefs while in others they identified their own sacred places, some of which have since been adopted in turn by native people.

Along with shrines on hills and near springs, shrines in fields, travelers' shrines, and shrines at the locations of tragic deaths, there are Hispanic shrines where extraordinary events have occurred. One of the most beloved of these is the Santuario de Chimayó in northern New Mexico. Built where legend says that a glowing light led a man to unearth a miraculous crucifix in 1810, a side room of the sanctuary is hung about with photographs and rosaries, crutches and tubes and other hospital paraphernalia, as tribute to the healing properties of the dirt from a hole in the floor. Before the arrival of the Spanish colonists, local Tewa people also

considered this dirt to have miraculous properties. Today, the Santuario is the destination of one of the largest spring pilgrimages in the Southwest. On Good Friday, thousands of *peregrinos,* or pilgrims—Hispanic, Pueblo, Anglo, and others—reenact Christ's journey to Calvary by converging on Chimayó, many of them walking all night, twenty-five miles or more to reach the sanctuary in the morning. As one man told the *Albuquerque Journal:*

> *I believe in prayer, I believe in faith, and I believe in this dust. And I'd walk it again. I'd do it for everybody, and I'd do it for anybody. I'd do it for animals. You name it, I'd do it. I'd do it for you, too.*

REBIRTH

"This morning I stood on the river bank to pray. I knew then that the ancient ones were wise to pray for peace and beauty and not for specific gifts except fertility which is continued life. And I saw that if one has even a small degree of the ability to take into and unto himself the peace and beauty the gods surround him with, it is not necessary to ask for more."

— EDITH WARNER

The southern deserts are fruitful in the spring. Mothers and children gather wild mustard and the flower buds of cholla cactus; rabbits and peccaries bear young sheltered by shrubs. Winter wheat ripens, affording a source of nourishment in the transition between harvests of corn and beans. In the

Interior, Santuario de Chimayó, shrine of Nuestro Señor de Esquípulas and El Santo Niño de Atocha. Built by local citizen Bernardo Abeyta in 1813, the santuario is sometimes called the "Lourdes of the American Southwest" by people of different faiths and cultures who consider it a place where physical, mental, social, familial, or spiritual disorders may be healed.

73

northern reaches of New Mexico and Arizona, it is possible to gather greens and even some wild fruits by this time. Regardless of the abundance of rain, birds, or flowers in a given spring, all Southwestern cultures celebrate the return of life at this season.

Catholics formalize spring's rebirth as the resurrection of Christ from the dead on the great feast of Easter (the word is related to both "dawn" and "star" and means "dawn light.") Centuries ago, Easter replaced Oester, a Teutonic festival of spring. In homes and churches today, symbols of incipient and newly born life abound: eggs, flowers, bunnies, lambs, and chicks. Easter is based on the Jewish feast of Passover; the last supper of Christ on Good Friday was a *Seder,* or Passover meal. It is celebrated on the first Sunday following the first full moon after the spring equinox.

The three days preceding Easter are the "Paschal Triduum" of Holy Thursday, Good Friday, and Holy Saturday, days that commemorate Christ's *passion*—his ordeal and death—during which spiritual preparation for Easter intensifies. Along with the pilgrimage to Chimayó, the Triduum is observed in New Mexico with great earnestness by *Los Hermanos Penitentes,* the Brotherhood of Penitents. Members of this society kept their faith alive during years of frontier isolation by means of charity and other acts that demonstrated the spiritual responsibility they felt for their communities. Many years later, Anglos encountering Penitentes in the remote mountains of New Mexico were aghast at their more extreme rituals and raised a hue and cry, driving the Penitentes into secrecy. The most

shocking to the newcomers were Penitente flagellants, who whipped themselves bloody as they sought to enkindle their own compassion and redeem humanity by sharing in the suffering of Christ. Though quite common throughout Europe in the Middle Ages and brought to the Americas in the sixteenth century (members of the Oñate expedition whipped themselves on Good Friday), self-flagellation had been virtually forgotten except in isolated outposts. Traditionally, Pueblo men and other native people also mortified their flesh in ritual scourgings as part of their religious practice before the arrival of Europeans, but the practice is not heard of these days. Those who once sacrificed their own blood now express their devotion to their faith and their fellow man through prayer and acts of service.

Eastertime follows Easter Sunday and is a liturgical season unto itself, a fifty-day period of celebration that balances the weeks of Lenten penance that precede it. In the words of ecclesiastical writer Mary Ellen Hynes: "It is the church's most ancient and most beautiful season. . . . days of blossoming orchards . . . of the great gladness of the awakening earth." At Easter and saints' days as well as according to their own calendar, Pueblos often stage what is called a *Tablita,* or "Corn Dance." In most pueblos, a crucifix or an image of the saint on whose day the dance is being held stands in a *kisi,* an evergreen shelter at one end of the dance ground, and the priests and nuns of the local church attend the dance as well.

Springtime represents birth, and the expected birth of a child is one of many occasions for what is probably the most famous of Navajo rites, the *Hózhǫ́ǫ́jí* or *Blessingway,*

75

Morada de la Conquistadora,
El Rancho de las Golondrinas.
Since an undetermined
point in the history of the
Catholic church in New
Mexico, members of the
Brotherhood of Penitents
have met in *moradas*
(Spanish for "dwellings"),
simple buildings in remote
places. The rituals of the
Penitentes developed not as
a way to impress outsiders
but rather solely for initiates.

performed often during the long Navajo summer. The *Blessingway* addresses the great questions of life, such as who we are, why we are here, and what we are to become. It teaches how to emulate the Holy People, with whom we "earth surface people" share a common essence and may endeavor to become. It is a path to hózhǫ—to happiness, peace, and plenty—and portrays how those in a state of hózhǫ act and relate with one another. *Blessingway* songs are the basis of the entire Navajo ceremonial structure. Every chantway ends with at least one song from the *Blessingway*:

> May it be beautiful before me,
> May it be beautiful behind me,
> May it be beautiful below me,
> May it be beautiful above me,
> May it be beautiful around me.
> Beauty is restored, beauty is restored.

Rabbitbrush flowers after summer rains in Bonito Park near Flagstaff, Arizona, San Francisco Peaks in background, and Tohono O'odham basket dancers taught by Danny Lopez, Maricopa Ak-Chin Nation, Arizona

SUMMER

SUMMER

Shiprock, Navajo Nation,
New Mexico, an important site
in the Navajo creation story

THE ONSET OF SUMMER IN THE SOUTHWEST USUALLY MEANS WEEKS OF WARM, DRY, AND RELATIVELY STILL WEATHER. BRILLIANT AND ALL-ENCOMPASSING, THE SUNLIGHT OF SUMMER SHIMMERS DOWN, LASTING LONGER AND LONGER EACH DAY. WINTER'S CHILL AND THE WINDS OF SPRING HAVE PASSED; THE AIR IS SHARP WITH resinous scents of sagebrush and pine in the north, of creosote-bush in the south. But the ground is powdery underfoot and colors and scents are everywhere muted by dust.

In the southern deserts, the harvests of winter wheat and wild spring greens are already over by the beginning of May; rabbits and birds have borne and raised their young. All living things prepare for the hot, desiccating first half of summer, many of them entering a state of *estivation,* or heat-induced dormancy.

In the uplands and northern reaches, birds make their presence known with sweet and earnest courtship melodies and brisk, territorial chirps and scoldings. Here, May means many hours of work preparing and planting the fields, interspersed with welcome rests at midday and in the soft evenings. Traditional farmers observe the sun's position at dawn as well as the emergence of key wildflowers to determine when the soil is warm and days are long enough to germinate and sustain beans, watermelons, squash, and gourds.

May also means earnest supplication for the rain that everyone hopes will begin after the summer solstice, the mid-point of summer, when all plant and animal life will be at the outer limits of survival. This time of year there are pilgrimages to holy mountains and offerings made at shrines. People tend springs, clearing away leaves and sticks and the other debris that can diminish the flow of precious water. In years when winter snows have been meager, priests and elders call for even more prayers, processions, and ceremonies than usual to beseech the heavens for rain.

Ancient calendars throughout New Mexico and Arizona mark May 1—a cross-quarter day—as the beginning of summer. For untold centuries, Pueblos have held Corn Dances around this date. Early Catholic missionaries connected these rites with the name days of saints. The Corn Dance at San Felipe Pueblo on May 1 is considered that pueblo's feast day, even though the official date for the Apostle Philip is May 3. Taos, Cochiti, and other pueblos also offer Corn Dances and bless their fields in early May.

European-Americans have long commemorated May 1 as an occasion to shake off winter and welcome the growing season. Schools and community groups sponsor maypole dances and crown May

79

queens with flowers in echoes of Beltain, an old Celtic fertility rite. Early in its history, the Catholic church dedicated May to the Virgin Mary to replace devotion to the goddess Flora, which was then prevalent throughout the Roman Empire. To this day, the faithful in Southwestern towns such as Clovis stage processions in Mary's honor on the first of May and place flowers at her shrines throughout the month.

Catholic processions take place on May 15, too, when priests lead Hispanic villagers carrying banners and bultos of San Ysidro to ask his blessing on farms and nearby streams. San Ysidro *Labrador* ("the worker") was a devout and joyful medieval Spanish peasant who, it is said, prayed and sang without ceasing as he plowed, planted, and harvested. Ysidro became the patron saint of farmers and farm communities. He is also remembered for his kindness to animals and his generosity to those even poorer than himself.

Bulto of San Ysidro Labrador, Chapel, El Rancho de las Golondriñas. Patron saint of Madrid, where he was born in 1070, Saint Isidore is greatly revered by those who work the land. "Saints are for the Spirit a place where he dwells as in his own home, since they offer themselves as a dwelling place for God." — Basil the Great

Although arid overall, the Southwest has two blooming seasons: the first when the soil warms and snows melt in spring; the second as the earth is soaked by summer monsoons. *Clockwise from left: Summer blossoms: narrowleaf yucca, Canyon de Chelly National Monument; brittlebush below Picacho Peak north of Tucson, Arizona; and claretcup cactus, Grand Canyon National Park, Arizona*

Wild Flora

Although New Mexico and Arizona may seem harsh and barren compared with greener places, there is actually great diversity in the native plants of the region. Their leaves may be dwarfed and their distribution sparse, but the plant families common elsewhere—from grasses to legumes to roses—are all present here, as are specially evolved drylands flora such as agave, cactus, and ocotillo. Because of variations in elevation and available moisture, the number of different species from these plant families is surprisingly high in the Southwest.

As the seasons unfold, people look for favored plants along low desert washes in winter and up in the cool mountains in summer. They gather purslane, lamb's quarters, and amaranth greens to eat fresh as salads and cooked as vegetables; yucca and ocotillo flowers to make into tea; herbs and chiltepine peppers to use as seasonings; acorns and piñon pine nuts to eat whole or ground into flour; and currants and hackberries, rosehips and juniper berries, wild grapes and wolfberries to nibble.

Recent studies indicate that native people fare better on what their ancestors harvested from the wild and from their own fields than they do on recently introduced foods. Today there is a high incidence of life-threatening, nutrition-related disorders such as diabetes and heart disease among the native people of the Southwest, but researchers have discovered that these conditions are greatly relieved by a return to traditional diets. Among the O'odham, for example, the beans from pods of mesquite trees were once a staple that provided high levels of protein, calcium, iron, manganese, and zinc. Flour made from the pods contains fructose—a form of sugar that does not require insulin—and soluble fiber, both easier on O'odham metabolisms than modern processed foods. The same soluble fiber that causes cactus to retain water in times of drought also slows the absorption of sugar in human bodies. In addition, analysis of native corn and other crops indicates that they are more nutritious than introduced hybrids, and that fresh foods eaten in season provide more vitamins than processed foods do.

According to radiocarbon-dating of the charred pits where they were roasted, the hearts of agave plants have nourished Southwesterners for at least eight thousand years. Rich in vitamins and carbohydrates, agaves grow wild and were also once cultivated throughout Arizona and New Mexico. Like so many other native plants, agaves have value not only as food but for their fibers, which can be woven into mats and twisted into cordage or sandals, and for their sharp leaf-points that may be used as awls and needles.

For Mescalero Apaches (whose name comes from a large species of agave called *mescal*), this wild bounty holds special significance in their arid, difficult land. In recent years, Mescalero people have revived the tradition of holding a communal agave harvest in May, culminating in a great mescal roast. The first plant to be harvested is sprinkled with cattail pollen and ancient prayers, then chiseled and levered from the ground with a sharpened stake. Harvesters chop off its long green leaves to expose the agave's heart, which can weigh more than thirty pounds.

Yuccas and eroding
granite boulders in
Aguirre Springs National
Recreation Area, Organ
Mountains in background,
near Las Cruces, New
Mexico. Days are long
and the sun is fierce
during the Southwestern
summer. Once, people
made the most of the
cooler hours of morning
and late afternoon
and rested near springs
at midday.

After hours of collecting agaves, the people bring their harvest to a central roasting pit, where a fire is lit that will burn all night. The following morning, the agave hearts are buried atop the coals under grasses and dirt, to steam for three days. These three days are a celebration, an occasion to reaffirm the bond between Apaches and the earth and to pass on wisdom from elders to the younger generation. There is feasting and the demonstration of traditional arts, and at night *Ga an* dance before a roaring bonfire. When the agave hearts are finally uncovered, some are cut up into sticky-sweet, fibrous chunks for onlookers to enjoy but most of the crop is kept for later events, especially the coming-of-age ceremonies so vital in the lives of Apache and Navajo women.

Various cactus are still important in Southwestern diets and traditions as well. Supermarkets and Hispanic restaurants offer *nopalo,* sliced-up pads of prickly pear cactus. Prickly pear also produce sweet fruits called *tunas,* which are consumed raw or made into syrups and jellies. In the early summer, cholla cactus buds are steamed and eaten as vegetables rich in fiber and calcium.

In late June, Tohono O'odham use a special long pole to knock ripe fruits off of lofty saguaro cactuses. O'odham eat these fruits whole or boil them with water to make syrup. The women may boil the fruit's heavy syrup into jelly or donate some of it to the roundhouse right after harvest. There, it is poured into a communal pot where it is mixed with water and fermented for two days and nights into a musty, mild wine that forms the basis of *náwait i'ita,* an annual ceremony to encourage the summer rains.

83

Dancers at Apache Mescal Roast, Living Desert Zoo and Gardens, Carlsbad. When traditional people gather to harvest and honor the earth's bounty, the celebrating often goes on night and day. Such occasions offer an important opportunity for young people to learn from their elders about the meaning and beauty of their culture.

Saguaro cactus and
ocotillo at sunset, Saguaro
National Monument.
"The tall mothers stand
there / The tall mothers
stand there / Whitely
they flower / Black the
blossoms dry / Red they
ripen." —O'odham
song transcribed by
Ruth Underhill

Elders sing rain songs while villagers dance and sing to aid its fermentation. Ruth Underhill transcribed several of these "songs to pull down the clouds":

The sun children are running westward
Hand in hand,
Madly singing,
Running.

The little red spider and the little gray horned toad
Together they make the rain to fall;
They make the rain to fall.

As the second dawn approaches, messengers invite neighbors to join in the drinking ceremony. A speaker who knows the orations reminds everyone to look after and be kind to one another and then bearers bring out the wine. Elders sprinkle a bit of it to imitate rainfall as they sing songs of the four directions. People state their relationships— "father," "brother," "friend"—as they hand wine to each other, singing until all of the wine from the roundhouse as well as that stored in jars at homes in the village is gone. General inebriation sets in—

Dizziness is following me!
Close it is following me.
Ah, but I like it.
Yonder far, far
On the flat land it is taking me.

—sometimes followed by vomiting in imitation of the longed-for, late-summer monsoon. This ceremony marks the O'odham new year, for it is the beginning of a new agricultural season in the southern deserts. This is the time to plant highly adapted crops that will germinate and yield a harvest despite the intense heat, thanks to the rain brought by the *náwait i'i* ceremony.

In many such ways, wild plants not only feed the body but nourish the soul, serving as spirit guides, messengers, and calendars. Reminders of the human connection to and dependence upon the earth, they play key roles in ancient Southwestern ceremonies. Certain plants represent the cardinal directions, powerful animals, and clans. Strong wild tobacco keeps people awake and induces visions during night-time rituals (as can the very dangerous blossoms and buds of certain other plants); tobacco smoke symbolizes rain clouds. Face- and body-paints on dancers often come from powdered plants. Holy meals of pollen, berries, and seeds are carried in "medicine bundles" so that their bearers may properly honor the forces and events they encounter in life. Twigs of sagebrush and other aromatic shrubs scent ritual fires, and the resin of brittlebush is burned as incense (hence its common Spanish name, *incienso*).

Native flora of the Southwest are useful in a practical sense as well, providing materials for buildings, tools, crafts, and the arts. For instance, designs painted with boiled beeweed on Pueblo pottery oxidize during firing to produce a distinctive, deep charcoal color. Pliable strips of willow, beargrass, yucca, and devil's claw are woven into baskets while plants from lichens to Mormon tea to rose hips are used to dye fibers to be woven into textiles of cotton (a plant domesticated in the Southwest since long before the

The plants of the desert provide many things to those who understand them: incense and flowers for ceremonies, pigments for paint, and fibers for paintbrushes and for weaving.
Clockwise from top: Brittlebush blooms in the Buckeye Hills Recreation Area, Arizona; Hano Polychrome jar and Pima basket, Museum of Northern Arizona

European arrival) and wool from sheep introduced by Spanish colonists. Wild gourds are dried and painted to make rattles for ceremonial dances.

Some plants are not cultivated but rather invite themselves into gardens and join those that are. Beeweed, sunflowers, and tomatillo take root and flourish with the blessing of gardeners, for they attract beneficial insects, rejuvenate the soil, and aid the planted crops in other ways that science is only now beginning to understand. People can benefit natural "gardens" in turn—the O'odham once tended desert oases by clearing up and burning fallen debris, reducing a source of insect pests while restoring nutrients to the soil. They planted shade trees and dug channels for water to reach them, thereby encouraging other, more vulnerable plants by extending the hospitable environment of an oasis out around its original spring. To the native eye, Southwestern wild plants are generous allies that will always sustain those who understand them.

CORN AND THE SOLSTICE MONSOON

June is a prayerful month, for it leads up to the monsoon rains that will nurse the fundamental basis of Southwestern agricultural civilizations. Although it is called *maíz* in Spanish (*maize* in Mesoamerica and in anthropological literature), the most commonly used name for this revered plant in New Mexico and Arizona is *corn,* an English term for "grain." Domesticated millennia ago from *teosinte,* a wild grass from the highlands of Mexico, corn is dependent upon people.

It must be cultivated in order to sprout, mature, and reproduce. For this reason, corn symbolizes the mutual dependence between humankind and nature.

Corn Dances acknowledge this symbiosis and pledge careful stewardship of the earth. They may be performed at any time of year but a major one is held at San Juan and other pueblos on June 24. Just as in winter, the sun appears to rise at the same point on the horizon for four days around the solstice. By June 24, villagers can observe that the sun is rising farther south on the horizon, meaning that days are definitely growing shorter. This is the feast day of Saint John the Baptist, a Christianized summer solstice that is still celebrated in parts of Europe with gift-giving, dancing, and bonfires, "a holy day for communion with the earth, sunlight and the beauty of all creation," according to Father Edward Hays. Saint John the Baptist symbolizes the Judaic laws and prophecies on which his cousin Jesus— whose birth is celebrated at the opposite point on the calendar—based his authority. For Catholics it is yet another occasion for a special Mass and fiesta, for Pueblos it is a proper time to honor the life force of corn, and for everyone it is a time to rejoice in the life-sustaining rains.

Southwestern corn comes in ears of all sizes and colors, each intended for a specific use and adapted to the precise environment in which it is farmed. Sweet corn is steamed or roasted whole, while kernels from other types are dried and popped, stewed as hominy, or ground into flour. Corn paste is wrapped in husks for tamales; dent corn is fed to livestock. In their long relationship with corn, native people learned it must be processed with an alkaline substance such

Corn growing at Coronado State Monument. "Birth: Young corn breaks ground / showered by rays of the rising sun. / They grow in happiness / become filled with warmth. / Silky tassels grow long / like my hair / in search of new beginnings. / Tomorrow / *itaha taawa* / travels the longest day. / With pipe in hand / we await our elders / who bring rain." (*Itaha taawa,* "My uncle, the sun.")

—Ramson Lomatewama

THE SOUTHWEST MONSOON

FOR THE FIRST HALF OF SUMMER, the Southwest lies parched and thirsty, already desiccated by gusty spring winds. As the days steadily grow longer, increasing hours of sunlight heat up the dry soil, which can reach a surface temperature of 180 degrees in May and June. Yet without clouds or humidity to keep the warmth gained by the earth during the day from radiating away quickly after sunset, nights are often extremely cold. Temperatures fluctuate wildly—up to fifty degrees from day to night—and a frost can occur in the high country any night of the year. Under these conditions, neither native plants and animals nor domesticated crops and livestock will survive for long, let alone flourish. Traditional people of the Southwest offer many prayers and ceremonies during this anxious time, in supplication for what the Navajo call *male rains*. These fierce downpours come from thunderstorms that usually begin soon after the summer solstice. They not only restore moisture to the soil but they also raise the humidity of the air, lessening the drastic swings in temperature over the course of each day.

Meteorologists call this season of powerful storms the *monsoon* (from the Arabic word *mausim*, meaning "season" or "reversal"). The monsoon season begins once the jet stream—which blows across the region from the Pacific during the winter—retreats far enough north to allow humid air from the Gulf of Mexico to flow into New Mexico and Arizona. Mornings are still crisp and clear but as the sunbaked earth heats this moist southern air, puffy, flat-bottomed clouds mushroom into the afternoon sky. Building into silvery-purple pyramids with flat bottoms that reflect the green or red color of the land, these thunderheads rumble and flick lightning like snakes' tongues. Black streamers of rain dangle from fleets of such storm cells that are each as much as a dozen miles across.

Early in the rainy season, the rain may evaporate before it reaches the ground, but later enormous drops of rain splatter the ground until it is soaked and the volatile resins of desert shrubs saturate the air with sharp fragrances. In contrast to the gentle, widespread, *female rains* of winter, the summer rains hammer the earth in a random pattern, sometimes leaving large areas untouched. Flash floods caused by thunderstorms occurring miles away can boil down even the slightest slopes into bone-dry country, spilling over the banks of shallow draws and arroyos. Altogether, the eight to ten weeks of the monsoon brings about half of the region's annual rainfall.

Evenings following these afternoon storms are astonishingly beautiful, with retreating clouds gilded brightly by the low rays of the setting sun. With the precious crops watered, the land and air refreshed, and the green flush of new life on the land, there is gratefulness, optimism, and celebration in the villages.

Rainbow and Pueblo Peak, Taos

as limestone, soda, or ash. Otherwise, a potentially disastrous niacin deficiency can result, a fact understood by medical science only recently. In one form or another, corn holds an honored place in native rites and introduced celebrations. *Piki,* the paper-thin, sacred food of the Hopi, is made of a very thin cornmeal gruel mixed with ashes and quickly brushed by hand over the scorching-hot surface of an heirloom piki stone, then peeled off and folded into a flattened roll which shatters into flakes that melt on the tongue. Households present basketry plaques of piki to the katsinas during plaza dances, and serve hominy stew to guests on ceremonial days. Pueblo priests bestow cornmeal as a blessing on fields, homes, and villages, on dancers and newborns and brides and the dead. Sand paintings depict cornplants, and Apache and Navajo blessings are signified with a sprinkling of corn pollen. At one time, communities of O'odham farmers made effigies of corn out of saguaro ribs and yucca leaves and sang songs over them for each stage of development—when the corn first appeared, was one foot high, then knee-high, showed tassels, had fully developed tassels, and finally when the corn was ripe. Although these O'odham ceremonies no longer take place, a few elders still remember and sing the old songs. And Hispanic households look forward to drinking *atole* (a hot beverage made of ground corn, milk, sugar, and cinnamon or chocolate) on holidays.

THE SOUTHWEST TRIAD

Anthropologists describe the basic indigenous diet as the "Southwest Triad" of corn, beans, and squash. After corn, the next most significant member of this triad is the lowly bean. Not only do corn and beans provide people with complete proteins, but growing these two together keeps the earth more productive as bean plants replace the nitrogen used up by corn. Beans depend in turn on the corn, climbing the stalks to reach more sunlight. Like corn, beans may be dried and stored for use all year, and come in a marvelous array of sizes, colors, and tastes. Pueblos originally cultivated various forms of lima beans, O'odham grew tepary beans, and now most join the Hispanics in raising pinto beans. Beans are acclaimed in many ways, from the great Hopi Bean Dance of early February to their place at every meal in some Hispanic households. Southwesterners know that cooking beans with the herb *epazote* makes them far more digestible.

The third major crop in this region was once squash, usually meaning hard squashes such as pumpkins but sometimes also taken to mean gourds and melons. Much less important than the other two these days, squash was once a symbol of bounty. Harvested in several varieties, it was cut into strips and dried for storage. The seeds were pressed for oil and ground for use as a thickener. Squash was a significant source of nourishment before so many other fruits and vegetables were introduced from Europe.

The earliest missionaries and colonists brought their favorite food plants with them into New Mexico and Arizona. They introduced fig, plum, pomegranate, and other fruit trees, nut and olive trees, grapevines, cabbage and other vegetables, lettuce and other fresh greens, lentils and chickpeas, herbs, anise, mint, and grains. These new crops spread all over the Southwest within a few decades.

91

"Food is not only a basic human need, it is also a sacred symbol: God in a multitude of forms and bodies. It is a focal point of fellowship and celebration. The cooking of food is also an artistic practice."
—Brother Peter Reinhart.
Clockwise from top:
Kitchen, Martinez Adobe, Taos; and squash, chiles, and corn at a produce stand near Española, New Mexico

Peaches were a great favorite among native people, as were onions and garlic. In addition, Spanish trading routes circulated food plants from points farther south in the Americas such as tomatoes, potatoes, and chocolate, as well as exotic flavorings: vanilla, cinnamon, and black pepper. In turn, the Hispanic settlers developed a taste for the wild chiltepines of the American Southwest, among the hottest of all chiles. The newcomers also brought rosebushes, lilies, and other flowers, establishing ornamental gardens that were strictly for pleasure in mission *garths* (enclosed gardens) and around their homes.

In good years, the monsoon rains sustain maturing crops throughout July and August, but the rains may be meager or never arrive. There were many lean years before the arrival of Spanish colonists. Villages often suffered when even good harvests of corn, beans, and squash dwindled over the winter. This changed to some extent with the introduction of wheat, which lessened the extremes of the former feast-or-famine agricultural cycle. In the warmer parts of the region, wheat could be grown in winter and harvested in spring, then ground and stored to be made into bread as needed. At higher elevations or more northerly places, it could be planted early in the spring and be the first crop to ripen. The ancient symbolism of wheat—as a grain that is sown across the land, gathered, then made into bread that is shared—is reflected in the custom of Pueblo, O'odham, and Hispanic households baking quantities of bread or cakes for special occasions such as feast days, weddings, and visitors from far away. These are often served as visitors arrive and given them as they depart in a bundle of food called an

itacate in Spanish. Perhaps the most familiar example of syncretism, or cultural fusion, as far as food in the Southwest is concerned is the ubiquitous "Indian taco," consisting of wheat flour dough fried in lard (both introduced), topped with beans and chile peppers (native), and lettuce, beef, and cheese (introduced), and finally, tomatoes (originally from points south).

COMING OF AGE

Just as a new year represents birth and springtime corresponds to childhood, midsummer symbolizes the passage into adulthood. It occurs when the land is lush and warm and ready to bear fruit. The time of year when boys are initiated into their social and religious responsibilities varies within Southwestern societies, but coming-of-age ceremonies for girls are most often held in the summer.

Certain pueblo villages present young women soon after the summer solstice. To prepare, girls carry out womanly customs such as grinding corn in stone troughs, washing their hair in yucca suds and arranging it on either side of their heads in "butterfly whorls" and dressing in the traditional clothes appropriate for adult women. They or their mothers make time-honored ceremonial dishes such as piki and mutton with hominy stew for their day of blessing and celebration.

Some O'odham still follow old customs surrounding this point in life, with variations according to village, family, and singer. The parents of a young woman encourage her very best behavior at this time, because it is when her adult character will take shape. They find her a godmother who will lecture her on O'odham virtues: to arise early in the day, be industrious and hospitable, and take good care of her future husband and family. Traditionally, this lecturing takes place over four days of seclusion and on each day there is a ritual bath. At long last, the maiden takes her place in her community and, says Danny Lopez, "The young girl's coming-out dance is *very* joyful." She dances next to the singer in the center of one line opposite another line of dancers. At one time the old ritual style of dance continued until dawn.

Especially in Arizona, *Quinceneras* are held for young Hispanic women who have reached their fifteenth year. In a special Mass held after months of instruction and acts of devotion, the girls are blessed and presented to their community. Usually, the girls' parents host a big party of dancing and feasting afterwards, an opportunity for the kind of open-handedness and hospitality known as *echando la casa por la ventana,* or "throwing the house out of the window."

Apaches and Navajos believe that an ancestral holy being—called White Painted Woman by the Apache, Changing Woman by the Navajo—was born into this world at the beginning of summer, to be reborn every year. For the matriarchal Apache and Navajo, the maiden's Sunrise Ceremony (*Na'i'es* among the Apaches, *Kinaaldá* among the Navajo) is probably the most culturally significant event of the year, for it is a reenactment of the one held for their holy female ancestor at the beginning of life in this world. It is a happy occasion that has become a summer

homecoming for family and friends who must live elsewhere in order to work or study. Some sponsors even announce upcoming ceremonies in the newspaper to gather as many well-wishers as possible. Over four demanding days and nights, the girl takes on the character of the sacred being, experiencing her power and becoming strong, healthy, and clear about her potential. Her family and friends bless her with cattail pollen and in turn request her blessing while she is in this miraculous state; her godmother prays over her as she guides her through the ceremony, literally shaping her with her hands. The details of the ceremony vary from group to group but all are rich in symbolism: a shell dangling on the young woman's forehead represents the one in which her divine self survived the primeval flood. She carries a cane she will keep for life, as it will retain the power evoked by the singers and concentrated by the good wishes of the community.

In Apache ceremonies, *Ga an* demonstrate the holy dances before a bonfire at night, and the diyin sing more and more of the creation story while the girl dances in the ceremonial tipi. On the final night she must dance until just before dawn. When the singers have "pulled up" the sun to shine on sun symbols painted on their palms (their timing is based on observations of the stars), she runs east towards the new dawn four times, circling a basket of sacred objects that is moved farther and farther away each time. Altogether it is an exhausting event for the girl, but as one mother said proudly: "after you have had your Sunrise Ceremony, you know your strength and you can survive just about anything."

Running

Running is important in indigenous Southwestern cultures. The races are strenuous; the racecourse at Zuni is over twenty miles long. In general, running symbolizes exertion towards spiritual as well as practical goals; in a sense it is a way to earn blessings through ordeal. Before the introduction of horses by the Spanish, people often covered the great distances of this region at a run. And they kept on running after that: messengers dashed from pueblo to pueblo on foot to coordinate the Pueblo Revolt of 1680 (their steps were retraced

three centuries later in August of 1980, by native runners from most pueblos as well as two Navajo youths). Hopis are particularly famous as runners: well into this century, Hopi farmers ran to fields remote from their villages and some who worked at Wupatki near Flagstaff would run eighty miles or so to spend weekends with their families at home. In Oslo in 1912, Hopi runner Lewis Tewanima became the first Arizonan to receive an Olympic medal, winning a silver in the 10,000 meter race.

Running can be the most sociable and unrestrained part of ceremonial occasions. Among the many forms of celebration on Pueblo feast days are races organized by age groups from toddlers through elders, with prizes to be won by the swiftest. During the spring ditch-cleaning season, kick-stick races enliven the work at irrigated pueblos such as Jemez, with betting and cheering and general revelry. These runs are also community prayers for rain. In kick-stick races, pairs of barefoot runners alternate in flicking a small chunk of wood ahead with their toes, to imitate the way floodwaters from rainstorms fling bits of debris down arroyos. Some runners sprint from sacred springs and shrines to lead rainclouds and other blessings into their villages. In western pueblos such as Hopi, katsinam themselves challenge villagers to race with them.

O'odham running traditions stagger the imagination, for even in the winter theirs is a warm and very dry climate. Like other Southwestern hunters before the Arrival, the O'odham once covered the ground at a trot and could run

Horses grazing near Shiprock, New Mexico. Before Spanish expeditions brought horses to the Southwest, indigenous people traveled great distances on foot. Farmers routinely ran to and from their outlying fields, while hunters had to pursue their quarry and carry it home unaided. Horses were a boon to native people, especially those who led a nomadic existence.

a deer to exhaustion. Footraces of twenty miles or more were popular as well as ceremonial events, with wagers made on who would win. Runners kicked balls made of wood or stone covered with sap to encourage the sun on its course. As traditional games are being revived, O'odham children are running again, in footraces, in their own version of field hockey for girls, and in a hilarious contest among girls to catch a boy who carries a pouch of money.

AWAITING THE HARVEST

After the summer solstice, work in the fields continues as farmers hoe the weeds around their plants, breaking up the soil to allow it to absorb moisture. Other tasks—among them the repair of leaky roofs and the tending of livestock—demand a great deal of time as well. Still, prayers and ceremonies must continue until the crop is safely harvested.

Soon after the summer solstice, with the blessing of rain delivered, all Hopi katsinam leave for their spiritual homes except *Maasawu,* caretaker of this world. This event is acted out in the elegant *Niman* ceremony or "Home Dance." New brides of the year are introduced and the first green corn crops are presented. Four days after this, the non-katsina season begins.

In New Mexico Pueblos and Hispanic villages, still more saint's days give rise to celebrations and ceremonies with increasing frequency towards the end of summer. Santa Ana holds Corn Dances on June 29, the feast of San Pedro, and on July 26, the feast of Saint Anne, mother of Mary and grandmother of Jesus. Taos presents one on July 25, the feast of Saint James or Santiago, an apostle of Christ and the patron of Spain.

MUSIC

"The Indians (and shortly thereafter, the African immigrants) were at once drawn to the music they heard from the Spaniards. And the Europeans were fascinated, and often influenced by, the astonishing, new sounds of other cultures."

— JOEL COHEN

With so many ceremonials filling the year, it is not surprising that music is an important part of life here. Songs are so essential to life that indigenous Southwestern cultures support individuals whose main purpose is to sing and teach those songs. They may be accompanied by drums or flutes, by rattles made of tortoise shells, deer hooves, or gourds with beans in them, or by the rhythmic steps of dancers, but the earnest words of the singer calling to the elements of the natural world rise clearly above everything else. Although these songs are ancient and formulaic, they still have an immediacy to them—their images are vivid and their summonings urgent as they cry out to the clouds, the sun, the Creator, and spirit intermediaries from katsinam to Holy People to the creatures of the earth. Because there were few if any stringed instruments in the Southwest before the arrival of Europeans (the one-stringed Apache violin may be an exception to the rule), the old songs were not constrained

Although most ceremonies are not spectator events, there are some public celebrations in all seasons where visitors may experience the singing, dancing, and traditional dress of the many cultures of the Southwest. *Clockwise from left:* Zuni turkey dancer, Gallup Inter-Tribal Indian Ceremonial; singer, Cinco de Mayo, La Mesilla, New Mexico; and Navajo singers, Shiprock Navajo Fair

in the same way as European music. Whereas the introduced music defines only half-steps, indigenous voices split notes into infinitely subtle sounds, and vary tempo and phrasing to suit the movements of a dance or the actions described in a song.

Today, it is possible to hear ancient songs in contexts such as weddings and special events at tribal cultural centers. Certain music must not be performed outside of ceremonies, but some Southwestern radio stations play traditional songs or contemporary compositions in the old style that are appropriate for general enjoyment, either interspersed with country music or on special programs with names like "Singing Wire." Among the most frequently heard are those sung by groups around a drummer, to accompany Navajo dancers. These are sung in Navajo, but one can often catch a familiar English phrase such as "pickup truck" or "job in town." Recordings of Pueblo, Apache, O'odham, and other tribal social songs are occasionally played on the radio, too.

One of the earliest examples of syncretism in the Southwest was the merging of music from Europe and the Americas, with Africa's influence present from the beginning because of Spain's long interaction with the Moors.

According to musicologist Joel Cohen, composers and choirmasters were usually trained in Seville but most performers and some composers were native. Spain introduced music for church that was generally of two types: the disciplined polyphony of the Renaissance and the more lively and spontaneous *villancicos* (carols) of the Spanish countryside. The latter incorporated local traditions and

Birds and feathers are important symbols. "As signs, birds relate to gods, act as messengers between men and gods, or stand as signals between man and man." —Hamilton Tyler.

Clockwise from left: Feather bustle, and two dancers with raptor talon, Taos Powwow; and Laguna turkey dancers, Gallup Inter-Tribal Indian Ceremonial

concerns and were often sung in local languages. They caught on and are still sung in some parts of the Southwest, as are old folk songs from Spain.

Regional styles evolved from the merging of European and indigenous musical traditions. *Waila* (from the Spanish word *baile,* or dance), also called "chicken-scratch," is a catchy sort of O'odham instrumental music with a strong polka influence. Bands playing accordions, electric guitars, saxophones, drums, and sometimes violins play waila at night-long dances. *Mariachi* music from Mexico is widely popular, both with old-fashioned seniors and increasingly, with teenagers in urban high schools who perform it as an expression of ethnic pride. Around Tucson car radios treat passersby to a full range of music in Spanish from marimba —with origins in Angola—to merengue from the Dominican Republic, to *norteño,* music from the northern states of Mexico. *Corridos,* or folk ballads, are composed on a variety of themes from legends of desperadoes to the everyday misadventures of the poor. There is also a growing genre of music inspired and performed by indigenous folksingers and rock-and-rollers throughout the Southwest using introduced instruments such as guitars and keyboards. As Joel Cohen concludes, the rich legacy of music in *Nueva España* is "a source of pride and joy for Americans North and South . . . and a witness to human possibility on our small, turbulent planet."

Pumpkin harvest and
Wheelwright shop, El
Rancho de las Golondrinas

Autumn

A U T U M N

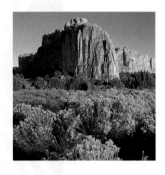

WITH AUGUST, SUMMER BEGINS ITS GRADUAL SHIFT INTO AUTUMN. RAINY LATE SUMMER DAYS AND STEADILY COOLING NIGHTS LEAD INTO SOFT GREEN MORNINGS, WHEN MIST SHINES WITH MINIATURE RAINBOWS ON THE BUNCHGRASS. THIS TRANSITION INTO THE NEW SEASON DOES NOT HAPPEN OVERNIGHT, BUT RATHER IN A

back-and-forth manner much like spring. There can be sudden overnight snowfalls in the mountains during the first week of September followed by scorching bursts of heat in late October. Afternoons in the canyons and southern deserts can be suffocatingly hot with cicadas clamoring along the watercourses, but gradually the land cools with increasing hours of darkness. The foliage of high-country aspens, maples, oaks, and cottonwoods changes color; bright fruits glow among the fading leaves of shrubs, trees, and vines. Chamisa and sunflowers—among the last of the year's flowers to blossom—burst into white and yellow blooms. Bull elk, strong from a summer of grazing and splendid in

new antlers, begin "bugling," challenging other bulls in a high, ringing whinny. Nuthatches form flocks for more efficient foraging and for communal roosting in tree cavities at night. Certain other birds group for their flights south, and the moist air fills with the butterscotch scent of ponderosa bark sharpened with a tang of fallen aspen leaves.

As a society we seem to be fleeing the seasons—moving south, seeking perpetual sun and warmth. Whether it is pronounced or subtle, however, summer does inevitably come to an end even in the Southwest. As the days shorten and grow cooler, the farmer's antidote for melancholy is hard and steady work while taking pleasure in the ripening of crops and joy in the harvest. Much of the work is shared, as lifelong neighbors move in groups from field to field. Few words are spoken as they labor; the tales and laughter come when they sit together to eat and rest. In the evenings there is time to relax, time to recite old, formal prayers and to retell ancient stories that remind everyone from toddler to grandparent of the great gifts of life, the land, and one another.

HARVEST

As corn, beans, squash, and melons mature, in certain pueblos it is time for ceremonies of the "old," pre-katsina, pre-Catholic religions. Alternating from one to the other each year, the Flute and Snake Dances begin at Hopi in late August. These ceremonies reiterate the proper relationship between the people and the land, encouraging the rains to continue while the sun ripens the crops.

A little later in autumn, the Hopi women's societies perform the *Maraw, Lakon,* and *O'waqölt* dances. In these plaza dances, the women aim at symbols of plenty, either shooting arrows at corn, bundles of squash vines or sometimes bean shoots, or casting the corn itself at symbols traced in cornmeal on the ground. In the Lakon and O'waqölt, they give baskets and pottery to the spectators, which has led to the general term of "Basket Dance" for

these ceremonies. In certain other pueblos such as Picurís, both men and women participate in Basket Dances.

In conjunction with the ripening and harvesting of various crops, there are a great number of feasts in New Mexico and Arizona throughout August, September, and October. Corn Dances in the Pueblos and special masses in Hispanic villages focus primarily on these harvests, but they also convey lessons about life handed down in both indigenous and Hispanic traditions.

On August 2, Saint Persingula's day, the Towa pueblo of Jémez holds a Corn Dance preceded by a great Bull Dance. The Bull Dance came to Jémez in the nineteenth century with the handful of Towa people from Pecos who had survived introduced pestilence and the raids of Plains people. While the Corn Dance emphasizes generosity and gratitude in humanity's relationship with nature, the Bull Dance evokes the power and wildness of the non-human world.

The feast day of Saint Dominic is celebrated on August 4 around the cross-quarter day, with a huge Corn Dance at Santo Domingo in which as many as two thousand indigenous people participate. Dominic was a twelfth-century monk who taught that not only the spirit but also the body is good. At Picurís Pueblo, August 10 is the feast of San

Corn at produce stand near Española. Corn symbolizes the mutual dependence between humankind and nature. It is the staff of life for indigenous people in the Southwest, and depends in turn upon a farmer's careful attention in order to produce ears. Pueblos cultivate corn in specific colors for ceremonies that honor this interdependence.

Cottonwoods with golden fall foliage lining the Rio Chama near Abiquiu, New Mexico. Autumn's arrival signals the end of the growing season and the harvesting of crops. In both Pueblo and Hispanic cultures, this culmination of the agricultural cycle is a period of feasting and ceremonies to reciprocate for blessings received.

Lorenzo, martyred in 258 when in response to a demand by Roman authorities for the "treasures of the Church," Lawrence brought the poor and sick. There is a footrace between the two moieties of Picurís on this day, as well as a Corn Dance. On August 12, the people of Santa Clara honor the companion of Saint Francis. Saint Clare practiced the same extreme poverty as Francis did, finding *her* earthly treasures in the simplicity of nature and the poor. At Zia and elsewhere on August 15, Catholics commemorate the Assumption of the Virgin Mary—the "gathering" of the mother of Christ into Heaven—with bunches of flowers, vegetables, baskets of fruit, and sheaves of grain around her image.

Isleta's September 4 feast venerates Saint Augustine, who turned from utter selfishness to the love of others, writing:

What does love look like? Love has hands to help others.
It has feet to hasten to the poor and needy. It has eyes
to see misery and want. It has ears to hear the sighs
and sorrows of others.

The September 2 feast of San Estevan at Acoma takes note of a third-century pope who maintained that what is in a person's heart matters more than official rituals. With a candlelit procession in Santa Fe and other towns as well as harvest dances at Laguna's Encinal Village on September 8, people celebrate the Nativity of the Virgin Mary, considered a model for those who wish to bring the presence of Christ into the world. Each village within Laguna Pueblo has its own feast day, but they all get together around September 18 —near the autumn equinox—to fête the Franciscan Saint

Joseph of Cupertino, a simple man of the seventeenth century whose faith was so great that he levitated, earning him the distinction of becoming patron saint of air travelers and pilots.

Because the O'odham plant after the summer rains have begun, their traditional thanksgiving, the *Célkona,* takes place in late October or early November. In the skipping dance that gives the ceremony its name (*célko* means skip) dancers skip two by two, holding effigies of clouds, water birds, rainbows, and mountains, all "dream symbols" of the rain. This is both a harvest festival and a petition for winter moisture: an outpouring of speeches, wagering on races and games, eating, and gift-giving. The O'odham tradition of generosity goes back to the old days, when the O'odham shared what they harvested to the point of never eating their own food. Instead, they would each give food to their neighbors until everyone had enough to eat.

THE AUTUMNAL EQUINOX

The northern shift from summer to winter accelerates around the equinox. Grasses have dried into tawny fluff, oaks have turned coppery, and the cottonwoods blaze with yellow leaves. The sunlight is gentle and no longer hammers down from directly overhead; the rains taper off as well. Blustery winds announce a shifting of weather origins from southerly to westerly. Summer has definitely fled and days seem to shorten ever more quickly, but the "harvest moon" (the full moon nearest the autumn equinox) sheds enough light for people to continue working out of doors well into the evenings.

In Las Vegas, New Mexico, the fiesta of San Miguel takes place in mid- to late September. Saint Michael, one of the three archangels, is petitioned for protection from evil during the coming cold and darkness. Once known as Michaelmas, the Feast of All Angels (Michael, Gabriel, and Raphael) is observed September 29. A day later, the feast of San Gerónimo (Saint Jerome) is celebrated at Taos with a Corn Dance as well as animal dances, a footrace, and a climb by "Black-Eye" clowns up a stripped spruce trunk to retrieve sacks of food that are then distributed among the people.

With the growing season for plants coming to an end, attention turns to the animal kingdom. Animals have borne and raised their young, and culling of their numbers may help remaining animals to survive as the supply of forage dwindles over the winter. The harvest moon is followed by the "hunters moon," a welcome ally of hunters during long, dark nights. Pueblos begin to perform animal dances again.

Being former hunter-gatherers, Apaches and Navajos regard autumn as the beginning of the year. During the second or third weekend in September, Jicarilla Apaches celebrate their *Go-jii-ya,* or new year, with a relay race between the two groups who live at Jicarilla. White-painted *Olleros,* called "potmakers" because of their historic closeness to the Pueblo, are associated with the sun and animals. They race against the red *Llaneros*—known as "people of the plains" after their bison-hunting ancestors—who represent the moon and plantlife. Should the Olleros win, people expect plenty of game in the coming year but if the Llaneros prevail, plant foods should be especially abundant.

Reflecting on the Pueblo animal dances, Peggy Pond Church wrote, "No wonder . . . we white people watch the Indian ceremonials with such envy. We have not lived long enough on this continent to mingle its earth with our dreams."

Clockwise from top left: Zuni turkey dancer, Gallup Inter-Tribal Indian Ceremonial; dancer, Taos Powwow; Zuni rainbow dancer, Gallup Inter-Tribal Indian Ceremonial; buffalo herd, Taos Pueblo

Either way, the racers help to ensure abundance and long, happy lives for everyone.

The Navajo *Ghaaji'*, or "dividing of summer and winter," is determined by observation of stellar constellations during the lunar month that corresponds roughly with October. It begins the season appropriate for the Mountain-way ceremony. At this time, blessings are also sung over seeds that will be planted in the coming year as well as for hunters and the animals they pursue. Traditional Navajos move from summer sheep camps in the cool mountains to winter camps lower in elevation during this time. Nowadays, younger Navajos from the towns come to help their grandparents with this move for there is a lot of work to do: chopping wood, packing up possessions, rounding up sheep, and cooking food for everyone.

On October 4, a great O'odham pilgrimage takes place. From points all over the Sonoran desert in both Mexico and Arizona, O'odham make their way to the town of Magdalena in Sonora, Mexico, for the feast of Saint Francis. In Magdalena, the identity of Saint Francis has become wonderfully confused over time between three men named Francis: Saint Francis Xavier, Father Eusebio Francisco Kino, and finally, Saint Francis of Assisi, founder of the Franciscans who replaced the Jesuits in 1768. When Father Kino died in 1711,

he was buried beneath a chapel dedicated to Francis Xavier in Magdalena, Sonora, Mexico. The O'odham began to make pilgrimages to Magdalena on the feast day of Saint Francis of Assisi. Saint Francis Xavier is considered to be a great healer. Some of the pilgrims require healing for themselves or others, or are fulfilling a *manda,* a vow made to the saint in exchange for his help. According to folklorist Eileen Oktavec, the O'odham regard this composite Saint Francis as their patron saint, the "Old Man" who looks after them and can be glimpsed around their reservation, stretching before he goes back to lie on his bier in the church. The annual pilgrimage has grown enormously. Some still make at least part of it on foot but however they get there, as many as ten thousand people—O'odham, Yaqui, Mexicans, and Anglos from both sides of the border—come for a multi-day fiesta. A few devout pilgrims make their way on their knees the last stretch past carnival rides, people selling beer and corn on the cob, and festive norteño bands.

October 4 is actually the feast day of Saint Francis of Assisi, who died on this date in 1226. Because of his affinity for animals, Francis is often shown with birds perched on his outstretched hands. Franciscan priests bless all sorts of animals that are brought to them on his day, from livestock

"Moreover they should respect all creatures, animate and inanimate, which 'bear the imprint of the Most High.'"
—*The Rule of the Secular Franciscan Order.*
From far left: Saint Francis with desert animals, by Apache artist Jim Stevens, c. 1940, Saint Francis Church, Maricopa Ak-Chin Nation, Arizona; statue, San Francisco de Asis church, Ranchos de Taos, New Mexico

Living close to the land, indigenous people are keen observers of the beings with whom they share it. Animals from butterflies to bears are often represented on or by objects, in some cases to imbue those objects with qualities of the creatures portrayed. *Clockwise from upper left:* Acoma or Laguna pot and Western Apache basket, Museum of Northern Arizona; and Zuni fetishes, private collection.

to dogs and cats, hamsters, gopher snakes, and parakeets. Nambé Pueblo celebrates the feast of Saint Francis with either a Corn Dance or an animal dance or both.

ANIMALS

> "What do we learn from Wren, and Hummingbird, and Pine Pollen, and how? Learn what? Specifics: how to spend a life facing the current; or what it is to perpetually die young; or how to be huge and calm and eat anything (Bear). But also, that we are many selves looking at each other, through the same eye."
>
> — GARY SNYDER
> "Reinhabitation"

Before the introduction of livestock to the Southwest, the only domesticated animals here were dogs and turkeys (Pueblo people also kept parrots and other birds for ceremonies.) Native people hunted wild game for meat, bones, and hides. Cottontail rabbits and mule deer were their most common quarry, but they also hunted pronghorns in open grasslands, elk in uplands and forests, and bighorn sheep in canyons and rocky country. There are still a great many of these wild game animals in New Mexico and Arizona, and one may spot tracks of coyotes, jackrabbits, badgers, skunks, bobcats, and foxes near springs and on dusty trails, too. Hawks and owls soar overhead, preying on tree and ground squirrels, mice, and prairie dogs.

But other wildlife has not fared so well. Prior to the nineteenth century, there were bears and wolves roaming the mountains and bison on the plains of New Mexico and Arizona. There were countless salamanders, frogs, toads, kingfishers, ducks, and grebes in the extensive wetlands of the region, and fish in the many streams and rivers before dams and cities eliminated much of their habitat.

All creatures are carefully observed by native people, who credit them with insights, abilities, and powers beyond the grasp of ordinary human beings. Many animals are found in stories and depicted in pottery, sand paintings, and ceremonial dances, indicating the awe and respect these cultures feel for them. Indigenous people pray and undertake ordeals for the success of their hunts, for they understand their dependence upon animals and the important place that wild creatures have in the world. The Catholic tradition of fasting from meat on Fridays began partly as a way to honor animals—which the Book of Genesis said were created on the sixth day just as people were—and partly a way to give thanks to the Creator of all living things. (See Source Notes for an explanation of the numbered days of the week.)

When Spanish settlers introduced chickens, guinea fowl, sheep, goats, cattle, and pigs to the region, these animals were a boon to people who had never had a ready source of meat. Chickens were especially important because their eggs became a handy source of protein. Although never a sign of prestige, chickens became important enough to enter Southwestern iconography. There is even a chicken katsina, called *Kowaako* for the sound it makes. Like the many other katsinam that represent birds, the Kowaako katsina dances and calls in prayer for the increase of nourishment for everyone as well as for rain.

111

Regional rock art suggests that before domesticated livestock arrived in the Southwest, bighorn sheep may have been the most prized quarry of Pueblo and O'odham hunters. Far less common than rabbits or deer, the meat of wild sheep is rich and savory. Today, sheep descended from animals brought by Europeans are the basis of staple dishes. Hopis serve a dish of mutton and hominy on special occasions, and a popular bumper sticker on the Navajo Nation reads: "MUTTON STEW—BREAKFAST OF CHAMPIONS."

The Apaches and eastern Pueblos who lived near the Great Plains hunted bison: massive, powerful, and dangerous animals. The Spanish brought relatively docile cattle, which as in so many other places in the world quickly became a status symbol here. The *vaquero* or cowboy remains a cultural icon representing strength and independence. Rodeos, tests of the skills needed to manage cattle, are still occasions for socializing and gaining honor in communities. But cattle require more forage and water than other livestock, and only a few can be raised on vast expanses of arid western range (in some places, federal guidelines recommend only one cow and calf per two hundred acres or more). Cattle, as well as sheep, attracted raiding nomads in the unsettled centuries after the Spanish arrived, and their need for pasturage led to conflicts over land use that continue today. Nonetheless, cattle, sheep, and goats provided reliable protein in the forms of meat, milk, butter, and cheese to people who had suffered malnutrition and even famine over the centuries.

Before the introduction of the pig, indigenous people did not cook with lard. Cooking oil mostly came from seeds of native plants. Today there are substitutions for lard, but for centuries after the conquistadors Southwestern dishes from beans to biscuits contained great quantities of it. In addition to being a source of cooking fat, pigs will eat a wider range of feed and put on more weight per pound of fodder than any other livestock except poultry, making them economical to raise for meat.

Most native stockmen do not slaughter their animals casually—meat is easier to buy at markets now—but rather for special occasions that call for obtaining meat with personal effort and sacrifice. Many rural indigenous and Hispanic households keep at least a few animals, for livestock is also valuable as a four-footed cash reserve that can be sold whenever there is a need for money.

POTTERY

Introduced livestock produced lots of manure, which was quickly adopted as a good source of fuel for firing pottery. Pottery had been made in the Southwest for at least a millennium before Europeans arrived, and is still one of the most revealing cultural expressions here. Unlike many other crafts, pottery is not limited in its shape or decoration by the materials from which it is made. Early pots were often in the shapes of natural containers such as gourds, however, and commonly decorated with patterns of parallel lines that some scholars believe imitate basketry.

Pueblo pottery is especially famous and each pueblo has its own tradition. For example, Taos and Picurís potters usually make unpainted micaceous ware while those at San Juan mix the same glittering clay with water and use it to fill

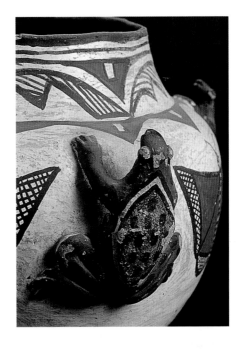

Clockwise from upper left:
Zuni Olla Maidens, Gallup
Inter-Tribal Ceremonial;
Acoma double-spouted
(wedding) vase; Zuni olla
decorated with frogs and
butterflies, with a concave
base for carrying on the
head; Zuni olla depicting
deer with heartline; and
Tesuque figurine, Museum
of Northern Arizona

POWWOWS

"Every viable Indian community has a powwow, and its components are simple: a people, a drum, and a cultural joy."

— GEORGE P. HORSE CAPTURE
Traditional Peoples Today

The word powwow is variously said to come from the Massachuset word *pauwau* meaning "council," or a Narragansett word meaning "shaman" or "power," or the Algonquin *pauau*, meaning a meeting of spiritual leaders for a curing ceremony. Today, the common meaning of powwow is a gathering of native people for celebration, especially dancing, drumming, and singing but also teaching, praying, and reinvigorating ancient traditions. Games, exhibits, concession stands, and sometimes a rodeo are often part of the festivities as well.

There are many powwows in the Southwest, usually in summer or fall. These echo the truces once called so that tribes could meet peacefully in order to trade. Participants camp around the dance ground for the entire event, which usually lasts for an extended weekend of four days. The encampment offers plenty of opportunities for people of all ages and backgrounds to meet one

another, talk, tell stories, play games, and form bonds of friendship that can last for lifetimes.

Powwows present an ever-expanding blend of customs from many different tribes across the country. While Native Americans generally endeavor to keep the traditions of their own people alive and pure, many also go to powwows to join in a growing sense of common purpose among tribal people. These celebrations are but one of several expressions of the *pan-Indian* identity today, along with a number of journals, political organizations, religious movements (especially the Native American Church), and broadcasts such as National Native News.

Spirited and flamboyant dancing is the heart of today's powwow. Dancers wear beautifully beaded and feathered clothing derived in large part from the traditional dress of Plains people. They compete with one another for awards based on their grace, athleticism, and passion, as well as their execution of specific dances. In breastplates and sometimes bustles, bells, tinklers, and moccasins, headdresses and facepaint, chokers, arm- and kneebands, men and boys whirl, leap, and stomp in "traditional," "war," "straight," or "grass" dances. Women and girls wear long, beaded, cloth or buckskin dresses and weave feathers or braid-wraps into their hair for the "shawl" and other dances.

The ornaments and designs on these costumes are more than decorations. They date from a time when Plains people went into battle wearing talismans for spiritual protection, and say a great deal about the life and relationships of the individual who wears them. And powwow dancing not only reinforces cultural identity—earning recognition and sometimes cash awards can encourage dancers to realize other goals as students, parents, and leaders.

Wa:ak Powwow, San Xavier District, Tohono O'odham Nation, Arizona

incised designs on their pots. Santo Domingo elders forbid the depiction of human figures or sacred designs on pottery, but Hopi *otsagavta* (pots) are often decorated with prayer feathers or storm patterns to encourage the rain.

Traditional O'odham pots were simple and graceful in shape, sometimes with boldly-painted geometric designs. Like many other Southwest potters, O'odham now make a range of wares, including some with human figures holding hands around the rims. Except for the Jicarilla who adopted ceramics from their Pueblo neighbors, Apaches were originally too mobile to find pottery of much use. After they settled down, some Apaches began to make large, practical jars and today make graceful pots for sale. The Navajo developed pottery too, but theirs is much simpler than that of the long-settled Pueblo people. It is distinctive, however, being coated with a pine pitch that gives it a glistening, almost oiled appearance.

Pottery has long been made for other than domestic purposes. Some Pueblos use ceramic containers in ceremonies. Individual pieces have been prized as objects of beauty. Zia people developed exquisite pottery that they traded for surplus crops of other pueblos. In fact, trade has had a considerable effect on Southwestern ceramics. Soon after Europeans arrived, native potters began producing soup bowls decorated with Spanish designs for the colonists (who also favored large, tan ollas from San Juan Pueblo). Ceramics continue to evolve today under the influence of a thriving market for Southwestern crafts.

115

TRADE

Trade has been a major influence on Southwestern people since time immemorial. Archaeologists find jewelry made of seashells at eight-hundred-year-old ruins that lie several hundred miles from the sea. Macaws—enormous, colorful parrots—were traded all the way from Mexico at least as early as AD 1100 (several dozen were found reverently buried with grave goods at Wupatki in northern Arizona). Projectile points of obsidian are found far from their volcanic origins; bits of turquoise leagues from their source. Sherds of pottery with the distinctive shapes and decoration of southern cultures lie scattered all over ruined villages in the north, and vice versa.

Old Taos Trade Fair, Martinez Hacienda, Taos. Today, many objects that have an ancient significance are being made for sale to interested collectors. In response to the market, old art forms have evolved in size, shape, color, and material, into fresh—though perhaps no longer sacred—expressions of native cultures.

One can only imagine the stories that accompanied these trade goods: stories of the vast ocean, of the stone-age cities of Mexico where talking birds were bred, of distant lands and different peoples.

Whether *puchtecas* (traders) made long treks themselves or goods were exchanged from one village to the next, it was a remarkably mobile network. Traders carried essentials such as salt, luxuries such as jewelry, and curiosities such as rare stones. People near one food source traded with those near another. Apaches traded agave to Navajos for piñon nuts, for instance. Pueblos exchanged cotton blankets, pottery, and corn with the people of the Great Plains for walnuts, buckskins, and buffalo robes, which were then traded all over the Southwest. The O'odham exchanged baskets and chiles to the north for pots, and it is said that they were cultivating watermelons obtained through trade to the south before Kino ever brought them any seeds. Groups of people traded customs from clothing styles to ceremonies with one another as well.

Even though they had no horses to bear them swiftly nor wheeled carts to carry their burdens, indigenous people were well aware of the wider world and many of its wonders. With the arrival of Coronado, these wonders increased. His expedition brought mirrors and blankets of unfamiliar workmanship; the friars brought candles, rosaries, and holy pictures. The Spanish soldiers brought horses, burros, and mules to the Southwest, which were immediately not only a great help in hunting and travel but also symbols of wealth and prestige that were highly valued in trade. (Horses also made it easier for raiding peoples to surprise villages and make off with booty, by-passing the trading system.)

In 1598, Don Juan de Oñate led his colonizing expedition of more than one hundred families north into New Mexico along an ancient Pueblo trade route. This became *El Camino Real de Tierra Adentro*—the Royal Highway of the Interior Land—for three centuries a vital link from northern New Mexico to Mexico City over fifteen hundred miles away. At first, the authorities in Mexico sent a thirty-two wagon caravan north every three years with supplies for the missions including the seeds of new crops, iron tools, sacramental wine, embroidered cassocks, and church bells. As trade with Mexico grew (New Mexicans were forbidden to trade with the United States or France), packed mules and ox-drawn carts brought patterned fabrics, pots and pans, musical instruments, glass beads, cutlery, and *piloncillo* (cones of brown sugar). In exchange, the colonists sent various crops as well as hides, wool and wool blankets, dried meat, and flocks of sheep. The course of El Camino Real is still visible in some places as a trackway worn into the land.

There were other important trade routes, of course. Trails still radiated out from all the pueblos, stretching over long distances to link them with each other, as from Acoma and Laguna up the drainage of the Rio Puerco to Zia and Santa Ana. Today's "High Road to Taos" was a historic route between Pueblos, and there were connections between unrelated groups as well. From Hopi, for example, trails led west to the bottom of the Grand Canyon and to the Havasupai, others went south to the O'odham and east to the Apaches, Navajos, and people of the plains.

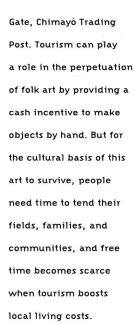

Gate, Chimayó Trading Post. Tourism can play a role in the perpetuation of folk art by providing a cash incentive to make objects by hand. But for the cultural basis of this art to survive, people need time to tend their fields, families, and communities, and free time becomes scarce when tourism boosts local living costs.

Trading was an important part of creating peaceful relationships between natives and newcomers, for each party had something positive to gain in these exchanges. However, although the Spanish crown forbade the trade of guns and gunpowder to indigenous people, these reached the Great Plains from French traders to the east. Guns changed the way whole groups of people lived. With them, the Comanches ruled the Great Plains by the early 1700s and plundered villages along the periphery of the grasslands. Jicarilla Apaches, who formerly spent summers on the plains hunting bison and winters camped near Pecos, Taos, and Picurís, began to stay in their camps rather than take the chance of encountering armed Comanches.

Nevertheless, trade with Plains and other nomadic people was important, and there were general truces between them and the Pueblos in late summer and fall to allow for the peaceful exchange of foodstuffs grown by the Pueblos for buffalo robes, dried meat, and slaves. There are echoes of this trading season in events such as the Gerónimo Day Trade Fair that is held in Taos at the end of September. Several Pueblos hold Comanche dances on their feast days: In midsummer, San Juan Pueblo men and boys carrying spears and wearing feathers and face paint stamp rhythmically from side to side then stop and shout, leading women and girls in patterns around the plazas.

For all these reasons, traders called *Comancheros*— for their willingness to meet the Comanches on their own turf—were considered dashing, romantic figures on the frontier. Hispanic and Pueblo men from Rio Grande settlements, they rode out into the plains to trade with any and all nomadic groups. They took manufactured goods as well as beans, corn, chiles, turquoise, and abalone shells, receiving buffalo robes, deer hides, and dried meat in return. Some of their encampments later became towns: Las Vegas and Tucumcari in what is now New Mexico, and Trinidad and La Junta in Colorado. Comancheros even crossed the daunting Llano Estacado to rendezvous at Palo Duro Canyon in Texas, and Santa Fe trade goods were common in North Dakota by the end of the 1700s.

Trade continues to be important in the lives of traditional Southwesterners. Traditional exchanges are still made from one group to another: Hopis provide other pueblos with specially woven belts; herbs and the minerals for various colors of face paint converge from everywhere in the region on villages preparing for ceremonies. People trade skills as plumbers or electricians or auto mechanics in exchange for help with the planting or harvest, or for horses or cattle or boxes of peaches. Makers of jewelry and carvers of wood take their work to trading posts in border towns or on their reservations to exchange for cash or for goods from groceries to washbasins.

WEAVING

One of the most vigorous examples of an old tradition sustaining people in the modern age is to be found in the Crownpoint rug auction, held every five weeks in the school auditorium of a little town in northern New Mexico. Those Navajos who live in remote hogans without electricity or plumbing can bring their work to exchange for cash that

Navajo rugs are made of wool from sheep introduced by Spanish settlers, colored with both native plants and introduced dyes, and created using techniques and patterns shared between Pueblo, Navajo, Hispanic, and others. *From upper left:* Wool and spinning and weaving tools; sheep near Chama, New Mexico; Sarah Natani, Navajo weaver, Shiprock, Arizona; and Navajo rug, Museum of Northern Arizona

they have no other means to obtain. Others may have full-time jobs, but they weave for extra income. Weavers also make rugs at least partly to stay in touch with their traditions and simply to enjoy the creative process. Some raise and shear their own sheep, clean the wool, dye it with flowers, roots, leaves, or lichens, and spin it into yarn to weave their rugs, while others buy their yarn.

In ancient times, it was Pueblo men who wove, spending long days in the kivapa making ceremonial garments as well as everyday kilts for the men, and shawls, sashes, and long, rectangular pieces of fabric that were sewn together to make simple dresses for women. They wove yarn spun from cotton fibers they grew themselves or obtained through trade with the Akimel O'odham (Pima) to the south, who themselves wove intricate textiles. At various stages Pueblo weavers sometimes wove designs into their cloth with yarns of contrasting colors, painted the cloth, or embroidered patterns along the borders. It appears that finely-woven cotton shawls became a form of tribute exacted from the Pueblos by early colonial adminis-trators, requiring that Pueblo men spend an unimaginable number of hours toiling at their looms just to stay out of trouble with the authorities. After the Reconquest when this tribute was no longer required, Pueblo weaving declined except in the western pueblos, where it is still done for ceremonial purposes today.

Anthropologists believe that the Pueblos taught the Navajos how to weave, perhaps while some Pueblo people sought refuge with the Navajos after the Pueblo Revolt. The Navajo say that Spider Woman taught them. In any

Originally, Navajo weavers made blankets to wear. Local traders urged them to make rugs for sale, sometimes using pictures— like those on the wall of Hubbell Trading Post—of popular patterns and colors to show them what to weave. *From far left:* Rug room, Hubbell Trading Post National Historic Site, Ganado, Arizona; Navajo rug, Museum of Northern Arizona

case, when sheep's wool became available, Navajo weavers began using it instead of cotton. They made large wearing blankets that were highly prized by nomadic people of the Plains. Navajos sometimes unraveled *bayeta,* a red woolen cloth imported by the colonists, re-spinning it to make yarn for weaving. They also used introduced dyes such as *añil,* or indigo, for deep colors. Eventually, Anglo traders influenced what Navajos wove, not only by buying weavings that had appeal for the market but also by providing specifications as to the pattern, size, and weight of pieces the weavers were to produce. With a Navajo loom, weavers must continually roll the completed part of their rug out of the way so that they may see what they are working on, requiring them to recall every detail of their rug's pattern to make it symmetrical from end to end.

In colonial times, another weaving tradition developed in the Hispanic villages of northern New Mexico. Often called the Rio Grande tradition, it is now centered in Chimayó. Unlike the native weaving done on an upright or vertical loom, the colonists wove on horizontal, harness looms. Although a few coarse blankets were woven in the 1700s, the expert phase of Hispanic weaving probably dates from 1807, when two weaving instructors were sent from Mexico to improve the quality of New Mexican textiles. In the early years, the patterns of Hispanic weaving were simple stripes of various colors. In the early nineteenth century, influences from Mexico led weavers to produce more complicated designs such as chevrons and diamonds— the so-called pseudo-Mexican style. Finally, Hispanic weavers began to adopt the far more sophisticated patterns

of the Navajos, possibly from Navajo servants. Today's Chimayó-style weavings mingle all three types: stripes, chevrons, and complex Navajo patterns.

BASKETS

Basketmaking goes back at least six thousand years in the Southwest, and is probably the oldest craft still practiced by the indigenous people here. Baskets were once very useful as lightweight containers for collecting everything from grass seeds to water (if woven tightly enough), but such collecting is now done with paper sacks, plastic bowls, and buckets. The old winnowing fan is no longer needed since flour can be store-bought. Toasting baskets have been replaced with wire screens, and cradle-baskets with canvas baby-huggers and plastic car seats. However, basketry materials—willow, beargrass, yucca, devil's claw—still grow both wild and cultivated, enabling indigenous people to make things of value using simply time, talent, and heart. Nowadays, baskets are generally made for ceremonial use, as gifts, or for sale.

Baskets are made on two of the three Hopi mesas. Women in the villages of Second Mesa make basketry plaques—and some deeper baskets—of coiled native grasses wrapped with dyed yucca strips. Though geometric, the designs on these baskets can be surprisingly elaborate with depictions of katsinam, corn and other plants, and abstract patterns. Third Mesa basketry plaques are entirely different, being woven rather than coiled, of rabbitbrush stems or sumac and bound on the edges with yucca. There are many ceremonial uses for these basketry plaques during both the

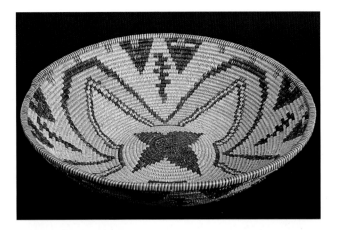

Basketweavers say that it takes a full year to make a basket: gathering pliable shoots and strips of bark in spring, drying flowers for dye in summer, cutting fibrous leaves in autumn, and finally, weaving the basket over the winter. *Clockwise from left:* Apache storage basket, Tonto Apache basket, Pima basket, and Western Apache basket, all from Museum of Northern Arizona

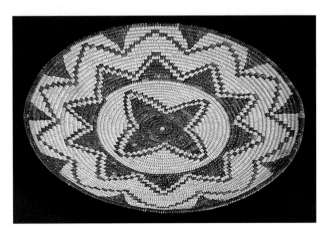

katsina and non-katsina seasons. They are given as awards in traditional footraces, used in weddings, and plaques heaped with cornmeal are carried around the village by the Crow Mother during the Bean Dance. In most Pueblos, women still make ring baskets woven of dyed yucca strips, too, which though simple are pleasing and very useful.

At the turn of the century, the O'odham were still making and using the *gího,* or burden baskets, large, lacy, conical shapes of agave fibers supported by pole frameworks. Traditionally, the Akimel O'odham used cattail fibers from the riverbanks and the Tohono O'odham used *nolina,* or beargrass. Both stitch their work together with willow splints and grow their own, genetically selected devil's claw just to have its long, black strips for weaving designs into their baskets. Today, traditional O'odham basketmakers are enjoying a renaissance. Some of them make miniature baskets as well.

Apaches are known for their "burden baskets," large, conical or cylindrical baskets now made mostly for maidens' Sunrise Ceremonies and additionally, for sale. Typically made of local materials such as willow or sumac, they are more tightly woven than O'odham burden baskets. The Jicarilla Apaches are considered the finest basketmakers in the Southwest today.

Navajo weddings would not be proper without a coiled basket in which there is moistened blue corn meal blessed by the hataalii and reverently shared by the guests. However, few Navajo women make baskets. The traditional wedding basket—a sunburst pattern with an opening that is directed to the east—is usually made by Paiute women for trade to Navajos as well as to visitors.

HEALING

Traditional people have always recognized that health takes many forms: a sound body, a pure spirit, harmonious families and communities, and a balanced relationship with the rest of creation. When any of these aspects of health is compromised, the rest are threatened as well. Within each of the cultures of the Southwest, there are many ways to cure physical disorders as well as means to prevent them. People use a wide range of regional plants—blossoms, leaves, fruits, bark, and roots—to reduce pain and fevers, to treat sore throats, common colds, and problems with the skin and blood, and as diuretics, stimulants, and sleep inducers. These remedies are commonly known and readily prescribed by herbalists.

There are also ritual cures, effected by healers who have learned them from other members of their societies or by shamans who have obtained their power through

124

Navajo Wedding Basket, Gouldings Trading Post, Monument Valley. Among the Navajos, wedding baskets are passed from hand to hand and sold or given to be used in a number of ceremonies, not just weddings. Although few Navajos make these baskets today, the need for them is met by San Juan Paiute basketweavers.

visions. People with such powers are respected but they are sometimes also feared. All of the societies in this book have traditional healers but they also believe that such a person's power can be turned to evil purposes. For instance, among the Hopi there is an old belief in a sorcerer-like personage known as a *powaqá*. Navajos tell scary stories about skinwalkers who cast malevolent spells, and rural Hispanic lore includes *curanderas* (healers) but also *brujas,* or witches.

Today, most traditional people rely on modern medicine but also undergo older cures. There is a Navajo hogan for healing ceremonies built into the Indian Health Service hospital in Chinle, Arizona, for example. The O'odham rightly consider many health problems—chicken pox, measles, and so on—to be brought by outsiders, and they seek conventional treatment for these "wandering sicknesses." But there are problems that have always been part of their collective experience called "staying sicknesses," which are much worse. These result from thoughtless behavior toward sources of power such as creatures or natural phenomena. When a person feels itchy or swollen or troubled by dreams, it is time to consult a shaman who will diagnose what impropriety was committed, such as the killing of a rabbit just for fun. A person can also do terrible things and not realize it, by unwittingly destroying a nest or otherwise interfering in the natural order of things. Shamans sometimes work over a patient all night to put things right, and then songs are sung that create an intense awareness of the violated animal's power and character. Ruth Underhill transcribed this one in *Singing for Power:*

Quail children under the bushes
Were chattering.
Our comrade Coyote heard them.
Softly he came padding up
And stood wriggling his ears
In all directions.

But health is seldom a private concern. For intimate, traditional societies, anything beyond a slight illness or injury suggests a soul-deep problem that may require the attention of spiritual healers lest it threaten the well-being of the group. The Apache and Navajo are particularly concerned with this sort of curing. For instance, should a traditional Navajo encounter an enemy or a corpse or spend time in jail, their family will arrange for them to undergo the *Enemyway,* a powerful rite of purification lasting one to several nights. Through this intensive regimen of singing, dancing, and prayers, the hataalii exorcises the patient's fear, frustration, anger, and pain from dealing with evil, restoring hózhǫ́ to the patient. Guided by prayers sung by the hataalii and accompanied by Holy People from the four sacred mountains, the patient relives the experiences of Monster Slayer, eventually overcoming the same forces that threatened the Diné at the beginning of their time on Earth. Dozens of well-wishers attend the final evening of social dancing and feasting around a bonfire while the hataalii sings over his patient in a nearby hogan. In a phase of the ritual called the *Blackening Way,* the patient is smeared all over with tallow and ashes in order to become invisible. To cleanse himself, finally, of the enemy that has tormented his dreams and sabotaged his efforts to live in harmony, the patient leaves the ceremonial hogan and casts his arms out four times toward the sun. Enemyways are often announced through local newspapers or on the radio to invite people of goodwill to be present for the sing. After the Vietnam and Persian Gulf wars, there were frequent notices of such ceremonies.

There are both medicinal and ceremonial ways to effect healing, but a great deal of effort is expended on preventing disorders in the first place. Running and prayer are both considered strengthening. Collective rites of purification both literal and symbolic take place often throughout the year, sometimes involving emetics, sleep deprivation, and fasting. Sweat baths are especially important in the traditions of Apaches and Navajos, to prevent problems as well as to heal them. One of the most dire afflictions is to be separated from one's community and from a sense of the spiritual, a sorry state readily prevented by participation in the seasonal round of work and games, celebration and ceremony.

STORIES

"It is so American. The belief that people can be
remade from scratch in the promised land, leaving
the old self behind."

— DEMETRIA MARTINEZ
Mother Tongue

In Anglo literature, the Southwest represents unbounded personal freedom, a place to reinvent oneself, to start over from scratch. This is not what it represents to the cultures who have lived here for centuries. To them, this is a land saturated with stories and with the moral obligations they illuminate; a landscape which is peopled with mythological characters and animated with events that illustrate great truths and values. These stories tell how to get along with ourselves, each other, and the world; how to hunt and plant and how to show reverence.

Such stories are anchored in place. The location of events can be as important as the events themselves. Native American place names are often a complete description of how a place looks or what happened there long ago. Traditional tales are often also connected to time, especially to a season of the year. Farming and harvesting lore is told on autumn evenings, for instance. Certain legends, especially those about creation, are appropriate during the cold months of winter when snakes, spiders, tarantulas, ants, and biting lizards are hibernating. Spoken aloud, they are experienced communally, not individually or privately as in books.

Stories from the pre-literate times of any culture are usually highly formulaic, told the same way each time so that they will remain accurate. Famous examples from the European tradition include the *Iliad* and the *Odyssey,* which were orally composed with clues in their rhythms and vocabulary so that no detail would be lost or mistaken. Vincent Scully considers Pueblo ceremonies to be in a league with the highest literary achievements of European civilization:

*The dances themselves I believe to be the most
profound works of art yet produced on the American*

Spider Rock, Canyon de Chelly National Monument. Natural features of the landscape, such as the dramatic spire of Spider Rock, can evoke a host of associations—with ancient stories, shared experiences, and moral lessons—in the minds of those whose forebears have lived in this region for many generations.

continent. They call up a pity and terror which only Greek tragedy rivals, no less than a comic joy, at once animal and ironic, that suggests the precursors of Aristophanes.

Pueblo: Mountain, Village, Dance
The University of Chicago Press

The journeys and encounters of ancestors and culture heroes find a place in the spoken literature of all cultures. Pueblos and Navajos tell tales of Spider Woman and her two grandsons, the Warrior Twins. O'odham stories are often old tales of shamans: their travels, heroic feats, and their role in creation; their Creator and Elder Brother (*I'itoi* among the Tohono O'odham, *Se'e'e* among the Pima) died but came back to life to look after them. In early Hispanic times, *los pastores* were tenant farmers who leased ewes from wealthy men and took them to high pastures to graze; both pastores and rich men became type characters in Southwestern *cuentos,* or stories, along with mystical curanderas and brujas.

In the Navajo language, as in others, one expression for "poor" means lacking knowledge of stories, teachings, songs, and prayers. Stories are the collective voice of a people; to be without them is to be without history, community, or identity: without a place to belong.

128

T H E   L E G A C Y

"We forget the deeper promptings that make us
what we truly are. And that is when we are truly poor."

— CHARLES BOWDEN, *The Secret Forest*

THEIR FIRST ENCOUNTERS with one another took place at a time when natives and Europeans alike were intensely aware of the passage of seasons. It was a time when people were so observant that they noticed an unfamiliar plant; when they were so intimately connected with one another that a rumor of strangers could travel hundreds of miles without benefit of telephone, broadcast, or newspaper. Impressions and intuition were powerful then, before the Age of Enlightenment and its insistence upon scientific proof. It can be hard for us—children of that Enlightenment and of its technological marvels—to appreciate intuition or the minute observations that guided daily life four and a half centuries ago.

From a handful of humble enclaves populated by relatively small groups of people, a powerful influence radiates across the Southwest. Why should this be so? Perhaps we find our own, long-forgotten selves in the people and the way of life here. And all of the things they create that we find so delightful are ultimately derived from the fundamentals: from earth, water, and sky, faith, hope, and community. Perhaps this is why they speak to us as they do.

Human nature being what it is, we try to keep our lives steady, stable, and comfortable. We cling to the notion that every problem can be solved and that hardship, pain, or

Mission San Xavier
del Bac, near
Tucson, Arizona

sacrifice can and should be avoided. We resist the pull of the seasons, using our technology to shut out the natural world and keep our distance from one another. But the price of insulating ourselves from the trials of life is to lose many of its joys. As the seasons unfold, they can remind us to look up and see the world anew, to encounter every day with awareness, gratitude, and love.

And so surely what is important to outsiders is not so much what a culture does, but why they do it. Life lived according to the seasons is life everchanging yet the same. To realize, "Yes, I remember how it feels to snuggle together and tell stories in winter, to see the first bluebird of spring, to plant, to harvest, to feast . . ." There is pleasure in this and sometimes, transcendence.

abuelo. Spanish, grandfather (or grandparent when pluralized as *abuelos*).

acequia(s). Irrigation ditches or canals.

adobe. A heavy clay, often containing straw, sun-dried and used as a building material, or bricks to be used in building; a building made with such material.

añil. An introduced dye used by Navajo weavers.

Apache. Jicarilla and Mescalero Apaches in New Mexico; Chiricahua and Western Apaches in Arizona.

atole. A hot beverage made of ground corn, milk, sugar, and cinnamon or chocolate, enjoyed in Hispanic households on holidays.

Basket Dance. The Lakon and O'waqölt, two of three plaza dances performed by Hopi women's societies in late autumn, in which baskets and pottery are given to the spectators.

bayeta. A red woolen cloth imported by Spanish colonists, unravelled and re-spun by Navajo weavers to make red yarn. ("Baize" in English.)

bulto(s). Figures of saints carved from gypsum, cottonwood, or pine.

Alvar Núñez Cabeza de Vaca. Spanish soldier who shipwrecked on the eastern coast of Texas in 1528 and went to Mexico City on foot.

Candelaria. Candlemas Day. Once called the Feast of the Purification after an ancient Jewish rite for new mothers, it is now celebrated as the Feast of the Presentation of the Lord, which commemorates Christ's appearance in the temple in Jerusalem.

cédula. Italian, document.

Célkona. O'odham thanksgiving, late October or early November.

cerros. Spanish, hills.

comanchero(s). Hispanic and Pueblo men who traded with Comanches.

corridos. Spanish, folk ballads composed on a variety of themes from legends of desperadoes to the everyday misadventures of the poor.

cross-quarter days. Landmark days that fall about midway between each solstice and equinox, important to farming cultures, denoting the change of seasons.

cuento(s). See **Los Pastores.**

Dine'é or Diné. Navajo, "the people."

Dinetah. Land of the Navajo.

diyi(n). Apache, medicine man.

Diyin Dine'é. Navajo, Holy People.

ejidos. Areas of land held in common by Hispanic and Native communities for grazing, water, and wood.

encomienda. A feudal system established for the Spanish colonies to exact tribute from natives of the New World in exchange for protection and for the purpose of converting them.

Epiphany. "The manifestation of divinity." Catholic feast day known as Twelfth Night or Kings Day, held on January 6 to commemorate the bright star that guided the Magi—the "three kings of Orient"—to the Christ child.

establicimientos de paz. Spanish, "Establishments of peace." Land granted to the Apaches by the Spanish colonial administrators for the purpose of converting the Apaches to farming.

Estebanico. Accompanied Alvar Núñez Cabeza de Vaca and two other companions on foot to Mexico City after shipwrecking on the eastern coast of Texas in 1528. Killed in the Zuni village of Hawikuh in 1539.

estivation. Heat-induced dormancy.

farolitos. Spanish, "little lanterns." Lights—once candles but now sometimes electric bulbs—in paper coverings, set along roadsides and around buildings in the Christmas season. Also called luminarias.

fête. To honor or celebrate, usually with a large, elaborate festival.

Ga an. Spirits from the mountains sent by the Apache Creator Yusin.

Ghaaji'. Navajo, "dividing of summer and winter," determined by observations

of stellar constellations during the lunar month corresponding roughly with October.

gího. O'odham burden basket: large, lacy, conical shapes of agave fibers supported by pole frameworks.

Go-jii-ya. Jicarilla Apache new year, celebrated in the second or third weekend in September.

hataalii. Navajo medicine man or singer.

himdag. O'odham, "way." In the words of folklorist Jim Griffith, "a constantly developing and evolving set of ideas and practices." *See also* **Jios himdag.**

hogan. Navajo dwelling; may be made of caulked timber, stone, mud, tar paper or other material and is usually eight-sided with cribbed roofs of logs laid over one another in increasingly tight circles.

Hohokam. O'odham, "vanished" or "all used up"; southern Arizona's early people.

Home Dance. See **Niman.**

hózhǫ́. Navajo, a state of wholeness and harmony with all things.

Hózhǫ́ǫ́jí. Navajo, Blessingway, a rite performed often during the summer.

I'itoi. The god (Creator and Elder Brother) of the Tohono O'odham religion. **Se'e'e** among the Pima.

itacate. Spanish, a bundle of food given in Hispanic households to visitors as they depart.

Jios himdag. O'odham, "God Way," and **santo himdag,** "Saint Way." *See* himdag.

katsina(m). Commonly known to English-speaking people as kachina(s), the spiritual beings and dolls of the Pueblo Indian religions. Differences in language sounds account for the different spellings.

Keresan. *See* **Tewa, Tiwa, Towa.**

Kinaaldá. Navajo girl's Sunrise Ceremony or coming-of-age.

Kino, Father Eusebio Francisco. Led Jesuit missionaries in the Sonoran Desert in the late 1600s.

kisi. An evergreen shelter at one end of a dance ground. During a **Tablita** or "Corn Dance," a crucifix or image of the saint on whose day the dance is being held stands in the kisi.

kiva(pa). Round or square ceremonial room(s).

Kowaako katsina. Hopi, Chicken katsina.

Lakon. *See* **Basket Dance.**

Maasawu katsina. Hopi, the original inhabitant of this world, the god of fertility and death, who does not return to his spiritual home with the rest of the katsinam during the **Niman** Ceremony, but stays with the Hopi the entire year.

mañanitas. Spanish, a song for birthdays or saint's days.

manda. Spanish, a vow made to a saint in exchange for help.

Maraw. A plaza dance performed by a Hopi women's society in late autumn. *See also* **Basket Dance.**

Matachines. Name variously thought to be derived from Spanish, Arabic, or Italian. Dancers in an ancient ritual introduced from Mexico.

mayordomos. Nominal leaders in a shared ditch system.

milagros. Spanish, "miracles." Miniature metal images portraying the needs of penitents.

moieties. Complementary tribal subdivisions (halves).

monarca. Spanish, monarch.

Na'i'es. Apache girl's Sunrise Ceremony or coming-of-age.

Ndee. Apache, "the people."

Niman. Hopi, "Home Dance" which takes place soon after the summer solstice. The blessing of rain is delivered, and the katsinam leave for their spiritual homes.

La Noche Buena. Spanish, "the Good Night." Midnight Mass on Christmas Eve. Sometimes called La Misa del Gallo (Spanish, "the Mass of the Rooster").

norteño. Spanish, music from the northern states of Mexico.

Luis Oacpicagigua. O'odham man who led a second Pueblo uprising in 1751.

olla. Spanish, jar.

Juan de Oñate. Headed an expedition to colonize Pueblos in 1598, and established a headquarters at San Juan Pueblo. Because of his methods was replaced by Pedro de Peralta.

O'waqölt. See **Basket Dance.**

O'odham. The Akimel O'odham are also called the Pima. The Tohono O'odham are also called the Desert Papago or the Papago.

palmas. Spanish, "palm leaf." Three-pointed wooden wands used by Matachines in their dance.

Papago. Tohono O'odham.

parciantes. Spanish, those who share in the water from a democratic ditch system. The nominal leaders are called **mayordomos.**

Los Pastores. Spanish, "the Shepherds," a Christmas play. In early Hispanic times, *los pastores* were tenant farmers who leased ewes from wealthy men and took them to high pastures to graze; both pastores and rich men became type characters in Southwestern **cuentos,** or stories, along with mystical curanderas and brujas.

peregrino(s). Spanish, pilgrim(s).

petroglyph(s). Images that are pecked in stone.

phosphene(s). Entoptic image(s) (produced by the optic nerve) that humans see when in altered states of consciousness.

pictograph(s). Paintings on stone.

piki. The paper-thin, sacred food of the Hopi, made of a very thin cornmeal gruel mixed with ashes and quickly brushed by hand over the scorching-hot surface of an heirloom piki stone, then peeled off and folded into a flattened roll which shatters into flakes that melt on the tongue.

Pima. Akimel O'odham.

Popé. San Juan man who led the Pueblo revolt in 1680.

Las Posadas. Spanish, "the lodgings." A Catholic procession reenacting Joseph and Mary's search for shelter during their journey to Bethlehem.

Powamuya. The Hopi Bean Dance, when the katsinam come to the Hopi villages to stay for part of the year.

134

presidio. Spanish, a small fort.

puchteca(s). Trader(s).

Pueblo. Spanish, "people" or "village." Pueblo with a capitol *P* refers to people; with a lowercase *p,* it refers to a dwelling or village.

Quincenearas. Coming-of-age for Hispanic women who have reached their fifteenth year.

rainhouses or roundhouses. O'odham structures in which men make village decisions and carry out ceremonies.

ramadas. Spanish, simple, free-standing shelters where people can craft baskets or pots or relax.

reredos. Spanish, altar screen.

retablo. Spanish, altarpiece.

ristra. Spanish, string.

rosca. Spanish, a ring cake with a doll inside it, a treat introduced to the region by Franciscan missionaries perhaps four centuries ago.

santero. Spanish, carver of holy figures.

santo himdag. See **Jios himdag.**

Se'e'e. *See* **I'itoi.**

Shalako. Zuni, giant couriers of the rainmakers who arrive at Zuni, pledging seeds and rain.

shaman. Healer or medicineman who uses magic to cure the sick, divine the hidden, or control events.

sodalities. Large societies among eastern Pueblo villages that probably evolved in order to maintain ditch systems.

Soyalkatsina(m). Hopi, Katsina(m) who visit the Hopi during winter solstice season.

syncretism. The reconciliation of diverse practices.

Tablita. Spanish, Pueblo Corn Dance.

Tewa, Tiwa, Towa. The three dialects of the Tanoan language group. Acoma, Laguna, Santo Domingo, Cóchiti, Santa Ana, and Zia languages are of the Keresan group; all other Pueblos speak either Tewa, Tiwa, Towa, Zuni, or Hopi.

tithu. Hopi, katsina dolls given to little girls by the katsinam spirit beings during ceremonials.

vaquero. Spanish, cowboy.

villancicos. Spanish, the lively and spontaneous music for the church introduced by Spain.

Waila. From the Spanish word *baile,* or dance. Also called chicken-scratch, a catchy O'odham instrumental music with a strong polka influence.

wickiup. Apache, temporary brush home.

Yusin. Apache, Creator.

135

MANY EXCELLENT REFERENCE BOOKS about the people of the Southwest for readers of all different levels of interest are available in libraries. I have listed several of my favorites below.

There is no substitute for personal experience, however. Throughout the year, tribes and museums sponsor cultural events to which the public is invited, and there are ongoing volunteer and educational programs involving traditional people that welcome support and participation. While out on a Sunday drive, stop and visit reservation shops and restaurants. It can feel awkward to wander into this parallel universe—especially since point-blank questions are considered rude and intrusive—but it also teaches us much about ourselves and reminds us of what being an outsider feels like. As Danny Lopez, teacher and cultural mentor of young O'odham people, said to me:

> *"People say they are interested in our culture, but there is a city of two million people a half hour away and nobody bothers to come visit us!"*

GENERAL

Bernard L. Fontana. *Entrada: The Legacy of Spain and Mexico in the United States,* Southwest Parks and Monuments Association, 1994.

E.C. Krupp. *Beyond the Blue Horizon: Myths and Legends of the Sun, Moon, and Stars,* Oxford University Press, 1991.

David Grant Noble. *Pueblos, Villages, Forts and Trails: A Guide to New Mexico's Past,* University of New Mexico Press, 1994.

Alfonso Ortiz, Editor. *Handbook of North American Indians*: *Volume 9: Southwest,* Smithsonian Institution, 1979.

Handbook of North American Indians: *Volume 10: Southwest,* Smithsonian Institution, 1983.

Edward H. Spicer. *Cycles of Conquest: The Impact of Spain, Mexico, and the United States on the Indians of the Southwest, 1533-1960,* University of Arizona Press, 1962.

Stephen Trimble. *Our Voices, Our Land,* Northland Press, 1986.

———. *The People: Indians of the American Southwest,* School of American Research Press, 1993.

APACHE

Keith Basso and Morris Opler, editors. *Apachean Culture History and Ethnology,* University of Arizona Press, 1971.

James L. Haley. *Apaches: A History and Culture Portrait,* Doubleday, 1981.

Chesley Goseyun Wilson, Ruth Longcor Harnisch Wilson, and Bryan Burton. *When The Earth Was Like New: Western Apache Songs and Stories,* World Music Press, Danbury, Connecticut, 1994.

HISPANIC/CATHOLIC

Arthur L. Campa. *Hispanic Culture in the Southwest,* University of Oklahoma Press, 1979.

Edward Hays. *A Pilgrim's Almanac,* Forest of Peace Publishing, 1989.

Mary Ellen Hynes. *Companion to the Calendar,* Liturgy Training Publications, Archdiocese of Chicago, 1993.

Roger G. Kennedy. *Mission: The History and Architecture of the Missions of North America,* Houghton Mifflin, 1993.

Alvar Núñez Cabeza de Vaca. *Adventures in the Unknown Interior of America,* University of New Mexico Press, 1983.

Lynn Nusom. *Christmas in New Mexico,* Golden West Publishers, 1991.

Marc Simmons. *Coronado's Land: Essays on Daily Life in Colonial New Mexico,* University of New Mexico Press, 1991.

Marc Treib. *Sanctuaries of Spanish New Mexico,* University of California Press, 1993.

NAVAJO

Between Sacred Mountains: Navajo Stories and Lessons from the Land, Vol. 11 of *Sun Tracks: An American Indian Literary Series,* edited by Larry Evers, Rock Point Community School: Sun Tracks and University of Arizona Press, 1982.

John Farella. *The Main Stalk: A Synthesis of Navajo Philosophy,* Unversity of Arizona Press, 1984.

Peter Iverson. *The Navajos,* Chelsea House, 1990.

O'ODHAM/GENERAL

Bernard L. Fontana. *Of Earth and Little Rain: The Papago Indians,* University of Arizona Press, 1989.

James S. Griffith. *A Shared Space: Folklife in the Arizona-Sonora Borderlands,* Utah State University Press, 1995.

———. *Beliefs and Holy Places: A Spiritual Geography of the Pimeria Alta,* University of Arizona Press, 1992.

———. *Southern Arizona Folk Arts,* University of Arizona Press, 1988.

Gary Paul Nabhan. *The Desert Smells Like Rain: A Naturalist in Papago Indian Country,* North Point Press, 1987.

———. *Gathering the Desert,* University of Arizona Press, 1985.

Eileen Oktavec. *Answered Prayers: Miracles and Milagros Along the Border,* University of Arizona Press, 1995.

Ruth Underhill. *Singing for Power: The Song Magic of the Papago Indians of Southern Arizona,* University of Arizona Press, 1938/1993.

PUEBLO

Edward P. Dozier. *The Pueblo Indians of Northern New Mexico,* Holt, Rinehart and Winston, Inc., 1970.

Alfonso Ortiz. *The Tewa World: Space, Time, Being, and Becoming in a Pueblo Society,* University of Chicago Press, 1969.

Joe S. Sando. *The Pueblo Indians,* Indian Historian Press, San Francisco, 1976.

Vincent Scully. *Pueblo: Mountain, Village, Dance,* University of Chicago Press, 1989.

Alph H. Secakuku. *Following the Sun and Moon: Hopi Kachina Tradition,* Northland Publishing in cooperation with the Heard Museum, 1995.

Dennis Tedlock. *Finding the Center: Narrative Poetry of the Zuni Indians,* The Dial Press, 1972.

Hamilton A. Tyler. *Pueblo Birds and Myths,* Northland Publishing, 1979.

SOURCE NOTES

PAGE   AUTHOR AND SOURCE

cover   Katsina dolls E3799, E3800, E3843, Museum of
Northern Arizona, Flagstaff, Arizona.

vii   Eric Polingyouma, personal communication,
summer 1995.

viii   Vincent Scully, *Pueblo: Mountain, Village, Dance,*
© 1972, 1975, 1989 by Vincent Scully. All rights
reserved. First edition published 1975. Second edition
published 1989 by The University of Chicago Press.

INTRODUCTION

1   Hano Polychrome jar by Fanny Nampeyo, E245,
Museum of Northern Arizona.

Epigraph, Carl Gustav Jung, Collected Works,
Volume 10, *Civilization in Transition,* paragraph
968, Pantheon Books, New York, 1964.

2   Dr. David Maybury-Lewis, Anthropologist, Harvard
University, "Anthropology Group Takes Activist
Stand to Protect Cultures." *New York Times,*
Tuesday, March 19, 1996.

Lance Polingyouma, personal communication,
spring 1996.

3   Zia jar, E1240, Museum of Northern Arizona.

4   Katsinam, E3757 and E3868, Museum of Northern
Arizona.

6   Danny Lopez, personal communication, spring
1996.

7   Pima Basket, E771, Museum of Northern Arizona.

9   Chesley Goseyun Wilson, *When the Earth was
Like New: Western Apache Songs and Stories,* © 1994
by World Music Press, Danbury, CT. Used by
permission.

9   Bryan Burton, in *When the Earth was Like New: Western Apache Songs and Stories,* © 1994 by World Music Press, Danbury, CT. Used by permission.

10   Mary Austin, *The Land of Little Rain,* University of New Mexico Press, 1974.

11   Cross-quarter days, Professor Bryan Bates, Coconino Community College, public lecture, spring 1996.

C. Daryll Forde, *Hopi Agriculture and Land Ownership,* Journal of the Royal Anthropological Institute, Volume 61, July-December 1931.

13   Epigraph, *Between Sacred Mountains: Navajo Stories and Lessons from the Land,* Vol. 11 of *Sun Tracks: An American Indian Literary Series,* edited by Larry Evers, Rock Point Community School: Sun Tracks and University of Arizona Press, 1982.

14   Wallace Stegner, *Crossing to Safety,* Penguin, 1987.

Roger G. Kennedy, *Mission: The History and Architecture of the Missions of North America,* Houghton Mifflin, 1993.

17   Both, Alvar Nuñez Cabeza de Vaca, *Adventures in the Unknown Interior of America,* University of New Mexico Press, 1983.

19   Marc Simmons, "History of Pueblo-Spanish Relations to 1821." *Handbook of North American Indians,* Volume 9, Smithsonian Institution Press, 1979.

Vincent Scully, *Pueblo: Mountain, Village, Dance,* © 1972, 1975, 1989 by Vincent Scully. All rights reserved. First edition published 1975. Second edition published 1989 by The University of Chicago Press.

20   Juan Mateo Manje in *Kino and Manje: Explorers of Sonora and Arizona.* Burrus, Ernest J., S.J., Jesuit Historical Institute, Saint Louis, 1971.

22   Zuni jar, E6733, and Navajo rug, E3153, Museum of Northern Arizona.

23   Alfonso Ortiz, "Introduction," *Handbook of North American Indians*, Volume 9, Smithsonian Institution Press, 1979.

24   Joel Cohen, Conductor, in Liner Notes for Compact Disc, *Nueva España: Close Encounters in the New World, 1590–1690,* Erato Disques, S.A., 1993.

WINTER

28   Larry McMurtry, "How the West Was Won or Lost," *The New Republic,* October 22, 1990.

Vincent Scully, *Pueblo: Mountain, Village, Dance,* © 1972, 1975, 1989 by Vincent Scully. All rights reserved. First edition published 1975. Second edition published 1989 by The University of Chicago Press.

30 Caption, Edward Hays, *The Ascent of the Mountain of God,* Forest of Peace Publishing, 1994.

Don J. Usner, "Hills shape the timeless spirit of Chimayó," *New Mexico Magazine,* October 1995.

31 Ruth Murray Underhill, *Singing for Power: The Song Magic of the Papago Indians*, University of Arizona Press, 1993; 1938/1966, University of California Press.

32 Dr. E.C. Krupp, Director, Griffith Observatory, from *Beyond the Blue Horizon: Myths and Legends of the Sun, Moon, Stars, and Planets.* Copyright 1991. Used by permission of Oxford University Press, Inc.

San Ildefonso: from the journals of Edith Warner, quoted in *The House at Otowi Bridge,* by Peggy Pond Church, University of New Mexico Press, 1959.

35 Ramson Lomatewama, "In Our Home," *Drifting Through Ancestor Dreams,* Northland Publishing, 1993.

39 Pico Iyer, "Spring Break, Here We Come," *Time Magazine,* April 1, 1996

41 Caption, James S. Griffith, *Southern Arizona Folk Arts,* University of Arizona Press, 1988.

44 Nina Otero Warren, *Old Spain in Our Southwest,* Rio Grande Press, 1962.

45 Richard Bradford, *Red Sky At Morning,* Lippincott, 1968.

Caption, Marc Treib, *Sanctuaries of Spanish New Mexico,* University of California Press, 1993.

47 Epigraph, N. Scott Momaday, in the foreward to *A Sense of Mission: Historic Churches of the Southwest,* Chronicle Books, 1994.

48 James S. Griffith, *Beliefs and Holy Places: A Spiritual Geography of the Pimería Alta*, University of Arizona, 1992.

Sacred groves, Sir James G. Frazer, *The Golden Bough,* Criterion Books, 1959.

Epigraph, quoted by Von del Chamberlin, "Rock Art and Astronomy: Navajo Star Ceilings," *Rock Art of the Western Canyons,* edited by Jane S. Day, Paul D. Friedman, and Maria J. Tate, Denver Museum of Natural History, 1989.

51 Jane Young, *Signs from the Ancestors,* University of New Mexico Press, 1988.

Caption, *Cathechism of the Catholic Church,* Doubleday, 1995.

SPRING

55 Pico Iyer, "Spring Break, Here We Come," *Time* Magazine, April 1, 1996.

Hopi katsina, E688, Museum of Northern Arizona.

Caption, Alph Secakuku, *Following the Sun and Moon: Hopi Kachina Tradition,* Northland Publishing and the Heard Museum, 1995.

58 Caption, Vine Deloria, Jr., in foreword to *When the Earth Was Like New: Western Apache Songs and Stories,* World Music Press, 1994.

Tohono O'odham basket, E781, Museum of Northern Arizona.

60 Gary Paul Nabhan, "Saving the Bounty of a Harsh and Meager Land," *Audubon* Magazine, January, 1985.

Jim Griffith, personal communication, Winter 1995.

63 Dr. Alma Garcia, Santa Clara University, (speech transmitted via Internet), Lockheed Martin Missiles and Space Cinco de Mayo Celebration.

65 Joe S. Sando, "Jemez Pueblo," in *Handbook of North American Indians*, Volume 9, Smithsonian Institution Press, 1979.

Governor Paytiamo, Public Hearings, Grants, New Mexico, 1986.

66 Pilgrims' Museum, Santiago de Compostela, Spain.

67 Carl Gustav Jung, Collected Works, Volume 10, *Civilization in Transition,* paragraph 969, Pantheon Books, New York, 1994.

Don J. Usner, "Hills Shape the Timeless Spirit of Chimayó," *New Mexico Magazine,* October 1995.

73 Bernardo Lujan, quoted in "Trekkers end procession of faith to dirt at El Santuario," *The Albuquerque Journal,* April 6, 1996.

From the journals of Edith Warner, *The House at Otowi Bridge,* by Peggy Pond Church, University of New Mexico Press, 1959.

74 Mary Ellen Hynes, *Companion to the Calendar,* Liturgy Training Publications, Archdiocese of Chicago, 1993.

SUMMER

79   Saint Basil, "On the Holy Spirit," *Catechism of the Catholic Church,* Doubleday, 1995.

85   Ruth Murray Underhill, *Singing for Power: The Song Magic of the Papago Indians,* University of Arizona Press, 1993; 1938/1966, University of California Press.

86   Ruth Murray Underhill, *Singing for Power.*

Hano Polychrome jar, E1317, and Pima basket, E771, Museum of Northern Arizona.

88   Edward Hays, *A Pilgrim's Almanac,* Forest of Peace Publishing, 1989.

89   Ramson Lomatewama, "Birth," *Drifting Through Ancestor Dreams,* Northland Publishing, 1993.

92   Peter Reinhart, *Sacramental Magic in a Small-Town Café* (extracted from pages xxii–xxiii). © 1994 Brother Peter Reinhart. Reprinted by permission of Addison-Wesley Longman Inc.

94   Danny Lopez, personal communication, spring 1986.

About sunrise ceremony, personal communication, September 1996.

96   Joel Cohen, Conductor, in Liner Notes for Compact Disc, *Nueva España: Close Encounters in the New World, 1590–1690,* Erato Disques, S.A., 1993.

99   Hamilton Tyler, *Pueblo Birds and Myths,* (text © University of Oklahoma Press, 1991), Northland Publishing, 1991.

100   Joel Cohen, Conductor, in Liner Notes for Compact Disc, *Nueva España: Close Encounters in the New World, 1590–1690,* Erato Disques, S.A., 1993.

AUTUMN

105   Augustine quoted by Mary Ellen Hynes, *Companion to the Calendar,* Liturgy Training Publications, Archdiocese of Chicago, 1993.

107   Peggy Pond Church, *The House at Otowi Bridge,* University of New Mexico Press, 1959.

109   Eileen Oktavec, *Answered Prayers: Miracles and Milagros Along the Border,* University of Arizona Press, 1995.

Father Cornelio Mota Ramos, OFM, *The Rule of the Secular Franciscan Order,* Franciscan Herald Press, 1980.

110   Acoma or Laguna pot, E6004, and Western Apache basket, E3112, Museum of Northern Arizona.

111   Gary Snyder, from the essay "Reinhabitation," collected in *A Place in Space,* Counterpoint Press, 1995, reprinted with permission.

As explained by Mary Ellen Hynes, *Companion to the Calendar,* Sunday is the first day of the week, for it is the day God began creation. Friday is the sixth day and Saturday is the seventh, which in the Jewish tradition is still observed as a day of rest.

113   Acoma wedding vase, E8587, Zuni jar, E5366, Zuni jar E6733, Tesuque figurine, E6634, Museum of Northern Arizona.

114   George P. Horse Capture, "Powwow: a powerful cultural revival," in *Traditional Peoples Today,* Harper Collins, 1994.

119   Navajo rug, E1843, Museum of Northern Arizona.

123   Apache storage basket, E1906, Tonto Apache basket, E794, Pima basket, E6884, Western Apache basket, E3111, Museum of Northern Arizona.

125   Ruth Murray Underhill, *Singing for Power: The Song Magic of the Papago Indians,* University of Arizona Press, 1993. 1938/1966, University of California Press.

126   Demetria Martinez, *Mother Tongue,* Ballantine Books, 1996.

Vincent Scully, *Pueblo: Mountain, Village, Dance,* © 1972, 1975, 1989 by Vincent Scully. All rights reserved. First edition published 1975. Second edition published 1989 by The University of Chicago Press.

129   Epigraph, Charles Bowden, *The Secret Forest,* University of New Mexico Press, 1993.

I N D E X

Page numbers in *italics* refer to photographs or illustrations

149

SEEKING TO UNDERSTAND the roots of her own culture, Susan Lamb majored in Classical Civilization at the Universities of California at Santa Barbara and Berkeley, and earned a master's degree in Aegean and Anatolian Prehistory at Bristol University in England. She joined the National Park Service two years later, endeavoring to connect her interests in the natural world and human cultures. Her career as a naturalist took her to Grand Canyon National Park in 1983, where she began to work among and interpret the people of the Southwest, especially the Hopi.

For the past nine years, Susan has led cultural and natural history study tours for the Smithsonian Institution, and has written numerous articles and books including *Ancient Walls: Indian Ruins of the Southwest, The Smithsonian Guide to Natural America: Southern Rockies, Grand Canyon: The Vault of Heaven,* and *Wildflowers of the Plateau and Canyon Country,* as well as several general interpretive publications for areas of the National Park System. She lives in Flagstaff, Arizona, with her husband, photographer Tom Bean.

SOON AFTER EARNING his degree in biology, Chuck Place received a camera as a graduation present from his parents. Plans for graduate school quickly faded as his interest in photography grew. Although initially a landscape photographer, Chuck eventually expanded into photojournalism. Working out of his home base in Santa Barbara, California, assignments have taken Chuck from the Mayan ruins in Mexico and outrigger canoe races in Hawaii, to orchid cultivation in California and numerous historic sites throughout the American West. His clients have been equally diverse and include *Time,* the Smithsonian Institution, and the National Geographic Society. In recent years, Chuck has shifted his focus toward book projects, including *Ancient Walls: Indian Ruins of the Southwest* (Companion Press/Fulcrum Books) and the *Smithsonian Guide to Historic America* series.